15 –MINUTE
JAPANESE
LEARN IN JUST 12 WEEKS

MITSUKO MAEDA-NYE
SHIZUYO OKADA

DK | Penguin Random House

Senior Editors Angeles Gavira, Christine Stroyan
US Executive Editor Lori Cates Hand
US Editor Kayla Dugger
Project Art Editor Vanessa Marr
Art Editor Shreya Anand
Editor Kingshuk Ghoshal
Jacket Design Development Manager Sophie MTT
Jacket Designer Suhita Dharamjit
Pre-Producer Robert Dunn
DTP Designer Anita Yadav
Producer Jude Crozier
Associate Publisher Liz Wheeler
Publishing Director Jonathan Metcalf

Language content for Dorling Kindersley by
g-and-w publishing

Produced for Dorling Kindersley by
Schermuly Design Co.

This American edition, 2019
First American edition, 2005
Published in the United States by DK Publishing
1745 Broadway, 20th Floor, New York, NY 10019

Copyright © 2005, 2013, 2019 Dorling Kindersley Limited
DK, a Division of Penguin Random House LLC
22 23 24 15 14 13 12 11
011–309121–Jan/2019

A catalog record for this book
is available from the Library of Congress.
ISBN 978-1-4654-7939-6

DK books are available at special discounts when purchased
in bulk for sales promotions, premiums, fund-raising, or
educational use. For details, contact: DK Publishing Special
Markets, 1745 Broadway, 20th Floor, New York, NY 10019
SpecialSales@dk.com

Printed and bound in China

For the curious
www.dk.com

CONTENTS

MIX
Paper | Supporting
responsible forestry
FSC™ C018179

This book was made with Forest
Stewardship Council™ certified
paper – one small step in DK's
commitment to a sustainable future.
**For more information go to
www.dk.com/our-green-pledge**

How to use this book

The main part of this book is devoted to 12 themed chapters broken down into five 15-minute daily lessons, the last of which is a revision lesson. So in just 12 weeks, you will have completed the course. A concluding reference section contains a menu guide, an English-to-Japanese dictionary, and tables of Japanese characters.

Warm up
Each day starts with a warm-up that encourages you to recall vocabulary or phrases you have learned previously. The time in parentheses indicates the amount of time you are expected to spend on each exercise.

Useful phrases
Selected phrases relevant to the topic help you speak and understand.

Cultural/Conversational tip
These panels provide additional insights into life in Japan and language usage.

How to use the flap
The book's cover flaps allow you to conceal the Japanese so that you can test whether you have remembered correctly.

Review and repeat
A recap of selected elements of previous lessons helps to reinforce your knowledge.

122   WEEK 12

1 Warm up (1 minute)

Say "(your) husband" and "(your) wife." (pp.12–13)

How do you say "lunch" and "dinner" in Japanese? (pp.20–21)

Say "Sorry, I'm busy that day." (pp.32–33)

SHAKOHTEKI N BAMEN DE
Socializing

As a business guest, it's more common to a restaurant than to someone's home partly practical—people often have long But if you're staying for longer, you may for a meal or a party.

2 Useful phrases (3 minutes)

Learn these phrases and then test yourself.

ディナーにいらっしゃいませんか？ *dinah ni irasshai masenka*	Would you like to come for dinner?
水曜日はいかがですか？ *suiyoh bi wa ikaga desuka*	What about Wednesday?
また今度誘ってください。 *mata kondo sasotte kudasai*	Perhaps another time.

Cultural tip When visiting a Japanese home, rem customary to remove your outdoor shoes at the doc for the host or hostess. Flowers, a bottle of wine, or your home country will be very appreciated.

3 In conversation (6 minutes)

火曜日のディナーにいらっしゃいませんか？
kayoh bi no dinah ni irasshai masenka?

すみません。火曜日は忙しいです。
sumimasen. kayoh bi wa isogashih desu

木曜日はい ですか？
mokuyoh b
What abo

96   WEEK 9

Kotae
Answers (Cover with flap)

FUKUSHU TO KURIKAESHI
Review and repeat

1 The body

❶ 頭 *atama*
❷ 腕 *ude*
❸ 胸 *mune*
❹ お腹 *onaka*
❺ 足 *ashi*
❻ 膝 *hiza*
❼ 足 *ashi*

1 The body (4 minutes)

Name the numbered body parts in Japanese.

- head
- arm
- chest
- stomach
- leg
- knee

3 Clothing (3 minutes)

Say the Japanese words for the numbered items of clothing.

- jacket
- tie
- pants
- shoes

2 On the phone

❶ 大和さんお願いします。*Yamato san onegai shimasu*
❷ グローブス・プリンターズのジャック・ハントと申します。*Gopross purintah no Jack Hunt to moshihimasu*
❸ メッセージを伝えていただけますか？*messeji o tsutaete itadake masuka*
❹ ミーティングは火曜日ではありません。*mihtingu wa kayoh bi dewa arimasen*
❺ ありがとうございます。*arigatoh gozaimasu*

2 On the phone (4 minutes)

You are arranging an appointment. Follow the conversation, replying in Japanese with the help of the numbered English prompts.

moshi moshi, Gopross konketshon desu
❶ I'd like to speak to Mr. Yamato.
dichira sama desuka
❷ Jack Hunt of Gopress Printers.
sumimasega, ima hanashichu desu
❸ Can I leave a message?
mochiran desu
❹ The meeting isn't on Tuesday.
wakerimashita
❺ Thank you very much.

4 At the doctor (4 minutes)

Say these phrases in Japanese.
❶ I have a pain in my leg.
❷ Is it serious?
❸ I have a heart condition.
❹ Will it hurt?
❺ I'm pregnant.

4 Words to remember (3 minutes)

Familiarize yourself with these words and test yourself using the flap.

party	パーティー *pahtih*
invitation	招待 *shohtai*
gift	お土産 *omiyage*

Read it You can now distinguish the three Japanese character sets and recognize some basic recurring words. Use the tables on pp.158-159 to look back over the lessons and see how much more you can read.

5 Put into practice (2 minutes)

Join in this conversation.

土曜日にパーティーを開く
のですが、お暇ですか?
*doyoh bi ni pahtih o hiraku
no desuga, ohima desuka*

We are having a party on
Saturday. Are you free?

Say: Yes, how nice!

はい、素敵ですね!
hai, suteki desune

ああよかった!
ah yokatta

That's great!

Say: At what time
should we arrive?

何時に伺い
ましょうか?
nanji ni ukagai mashohka

Instructions
Each exercise is numbered
and introduced with
instructions. In some
cases, more information is
given about the language
point being covered.

Read it
These panels help you
understand how the
Japanese script works,
present useful signs,
and give tips for
deciphering Japanese
characters.

空港 *ku-koh*
airport

Read it Here's another
example of two *kanji*
characters combining to
make a separate meaning:
空 (*ku*, sky) +
港 (*koh*, port).

Text styles
Japanese script
and easy-to-read
pronunciation are
shown, along with
the English translation.

招待者
shohtai sha
hostess

お客
okyaku
guest

ご招待ありがとう
ございます。
goshohtai arigatoh gozaimasu
Thank you for inviting us.

はい、素敵ですね!
hai, suteki desune

Yes, how nice!

ご主人もご一緒に。
goshujin mo goissho ni

Please bring your husband.

何時に伺いましょうか?
nanji ni ukagai mashohka

At what time should
we arrive?

In conversation
Illustrated dialogues
reflecting how
vocabulary and
phrases are used in
everyday situations
appear throughout
the book.

Say it
In these exercises,
you are asked to
apply what you
have learned using
different vocabulary.

5 Say it (2 minutes)

Do you have any single rooms?

For two nights.

Is dinner included?

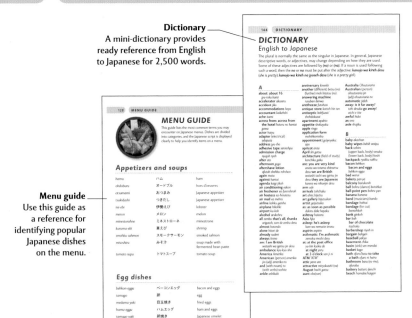

Dictionary
A mini-dictionary provides
ready reference from English
to Japanese for 2,500 words.

Menu guide
Use this guide as
a reference for
identifying popular
Japanese dishes
on the menu.

Pronunciation guide

Most Japanese sounds will already be familiar to you, and the pronunciation guide given for all words and phrases in *15-Minute Japanese* is designed to be natural to read. However, a few sounds require additional explanation:

r	a Japanese *r* is pronounced like a cross between an English *r* and *l*
ih	*ee* as in sh**ee**p
eh	long *eh*, like a longer version of the sound in th**ey**
oh	long *o* as in m**o**tor
final *u*	the final *u* written on the end of words, such as *desu* (is/are) and *(ga/a) arimasu* (there is/are), is only slightly pronounced and often sounds more like a double letter (e.g. *dess*).

The Japanese language is based on syllables rather than individual letters. Each syllable is pronounced with roughly equal stress.

How to use the audio app

All the numbered exercises in each lesson, apart from the Warm ups at the beginning and the Say it exercises at the end, have recorded audio, available via a free app. The app also includes a function to record yourself and listen to yourself alongside native speakers.

To start using the audio with the book, first download the **DK 15-Minute Language Course** app on your smartphone or tablet from the App Store or Google Play. Open the app and scan the QR code on the back of this book to add it to your Library. As soon as the QR code is recognized, the audio will download.

There are two ways in which you can use the audio. The first is to read through your 15-minute lessons using the book only, and then go back and work with the audio and the book together, repeating the text in the gaps provided and then recording yourself. Or you can combine the book and the audio right from the beginning, pausing the app to read the instructions on the page as you need to. Try to say the words aloud, and practice enunciating properly. Detailed instructions on how to use the app are available from the menu bar in the app.

Remember that repetition is vital to language learning. The more often you listen to a conversation or repeat an oral exercise, the more the language will sink in.

Menu, Help/How to Use, Your Library

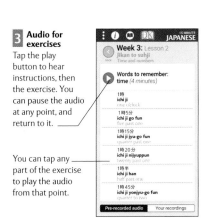

1 Getting started
The list of weeks will open when the audio has been downloaded. From here, you can tap into each week's lessons.

When all the lessons in a week have been completed, the week button will be filled with color and show a check mark, so you can track your progress.

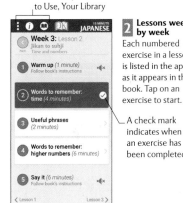

2 Lessons week by week
Each numbered exercise in a lesson is listed in the app as it appears in the book. Tap on an exercise to start.

A check mark indicates when an exercise has been completed.

3 Audio for exercises
Tap the play button to hear instructions, then the exercise. You can pause the audio at any point, and return to it.

You can tap any part of the exercise to play the audio from that point.

4 Record yourself
When you are in the *Your recordings* screen, you can record yourself reading the words or participating in the conversations with native speakers, then listen back (and rerecord if desired).

Add recording
Play recording

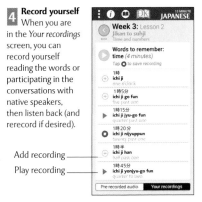

1 **Warm up** (1 minute)

The Warm Up panel appears at the beginning of each topic. Use it to reinforce what you have already learned and to prepare yourself for moving ahead with the new subject.

KONNICHIWA
Hello

The Japanese bow is famous: the lower the bow, the more respectful. Traditionally, there would not be any contact in the form of a handshake or kisses. With the increasing Western influence, the Japanese now often shake hands, sometimes bowing at the same time, especially when meeting foreigners.

2 **Words to remember** (6 minutes)

こんにちは。
konnichiwa
Hello!

Say these expressions aloud. Hide the text on the left with the cover flap and try to remember the Japanese for each. Check your answers.

おはようございます。 *ohayo gozaimasu*	Good morning.
こんばんは。 *konbanwa*	Good evening.
私の名前は...です。 *watashi no namae wa...desu*	My name is ...
どうぞ、よろしく。 *dohzo yoroshiku*	Pleased to meet you.
さようなら。 *sayohnara*	Goodbye. (formal)
さよなら。 *sayonara*	Goodbye. (informal)
ではまたあした。 *dewa mata ashita*	See you tomorrow.

3 **In conversation: formal** (3 minutes)

こんにちは。
私の名前は岡田です。
konnichiwa. watashi no namae wa Okada desu

Hello. My name is Okada.

こんにちは。私の名前はロバート・バーカーです。
konnichiwa. watashi no namae wa Robahto Barker desu

Hello. My name is Robert Barker.

どうぞ、よろしく。
dohzo yoroshiku

Pleased to meet you.

4 Put into practice (2 minutes)

Join in this conversation. Read the Japanese beside the pictures on the left and then follow the instructions to make your reply. Then test yourself by concealing the answers with the cover flap.

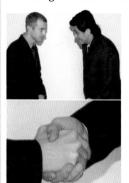

こんばんは。
konbanwa

こんばんは。
konbanwa

Good evening.

Say: Good evening.

私の名前は前田美樹朗です。
watashi no namae wa Maeda Mikiro desu

My name is Maeda Mikiro.

Say: Pleased to meet you, Maeda-san.

どうぞ、よろしく前田さん。
dohzo yoroshiku Maeda-san

Conversational tip The Japanese usually introduce themselves using either just the family name—Okada—or the family name followed by the first name—Maeda Mikiro. But they are used to hearing Western names the other way: Robert Barker. It's not common to ask someone their name directly, so listen carefully to the introductions. When talking to/about others, you should add the honorific *san*, but don't use *san* when talking about yourself. Levels of formality are built into the Japanese language, and it takes time to acquire a feel for this. This program will introduce you to polite, but not overformal, Japanese.

5 In conversation: informal (3 minutes)

ではまたあした?
dewa mata ashita

See you tomorrow?

はい、ではまたあした。
Hai, dewa mata ashita

Yes, see you tomorrow.

さよなら。
sayonara

Goodbye.

WATASHI NO KAZOKU
My family

1 Warm up (1 minute)

Say "hello" and "goodbye" in Japanese. (pp.8-9)

Now say "My name is ...." (pp.8-9)

Say "Pleased to meet you, Maeda-san." (pp.8-9)

Japanese has two sets of vocabulary for family members, depending on whether you are talking about your own or someone else's. This lesson concentrates on talking about your own family. As **chichi** means _my_ father, **musume** _my_ daughter, etc., there is no need for a separate word meaning _my_.

2 Match and repeat (5 minutes)

Look at the numbered family members in this scene and match them with the vocabulary list at the side. Read the Japanese words aloud. Now, hide the list with the cover flap and test yourself.

❶ 祖母
   sobo

❷ 祖父
   sofu

❸ 父
   chichi

❹ 母
   haha

❺ 息子
   musuko

❻ 娘
   musume

❶ my grandmother

❷ my grandfather

❸ my father

❻ my daughter

❺ my son

❹ my mother

Conversational tip Japanese distinguishes between little and big sister or brother. You will find all the relevant words in section 4. The word **kyohdai** (siblings) is used to refer to your brothers and sisters as a group: **kyohdai ga yo nin imasu** (I have four siblings).

3 Words to remember: numbers (4 minutes)

The numbers opposite are "general" numerals used for mathematical functions or for money. The Japanese use a system of "classifiers" to count specific things. These vary with the nature of what is being counted—for example, its shape (long and thin, round and flat, etc.). A beginner can get away with using the general numbers, but it's useful to know the classifiers used for people to talk about your family:

一人	hitori	1 person
二人	futari	2 people
三人	san nin	3 people
四人	yo nin	4 people
五人	go nin	5 people
六人	roku nin	6 people
七人	shichi nin	7 people
八人	hachi nin	8 people
九人	kyu nin	9 people
十人	jyu nin	10 people

one	一	ichi
two	二	ni
three	三	san
four	四	shi/yon
five	五	go
six	六	roku
seven	七	shichi/nana
eight	八	hachi
nine	九	kyu
ten	十	jyu
eleven	十一	jyu-ichi
twelve	十二	jyu-ni

4 Words to remember: relatives (5 minutes)

妻
tsuma
my wife

夫
otto
my husband

結婚しています。
kekkon shite imasu
I'm married.

Look at these words and say them aloud. Hide the text on the right with the cover flap and try to remember the Japanese. Check your answers and repeat if necessary. Then practice the phrases below.

my big sister/ my little sister	姉/妹 *ane/imohto*
my big brother/ my little brother	兄/弟 *ani/otohto*
my siblings	兄弟 *kyohdai*
This is my wife.	これは私の妻です。 *kore wa watashi no tsuma desu*
I have four children.	子供が四人います。 *kodomo ga yo nin imasu*
We have two daughters.	娘が二人います。 *musume ga futari imasu*

1 Warm up (1 minute)

Say the Japanese for as many members of (your own) family as you can. (pp.10-11)

Say "I have two sons." (pp.10-11)

SHINSEKI
Your relatives

Japanese has more respectful terms when referring to someone else's relatives. *Your mother* is **okahsan**; *your* is understood. Likewise, it's not common to use *his* or *her*, but to specify a name (+ **san**)–for example, **kore wa Akkiko-san no otohsan desu** (*This is her [Akiko's] father*).

2 Words to remember (5 minutes)

There are different words for referring to family members in Japanese. Here are the more respectful terms for someone else's family.

お母さん *okahsan*	mother	
お父さん *otohsan*	father	
息子さん *musuko san*	son	
娘さん *musume san*	daughter	
奥さん *okusan*	wife	
ご主人 *goshujin*	husband	
子供さん *kodomo san*	children	
ご兄弟 *go kyohdai*	siblings	

これはお母さんですか?
kore wa okahsan desuka
Is this your mother?

3 In conversation (4 minutes)

これはご主人ですか?
kore wa goshujin desuka

Is this your husband?

そうです。そして
これは私の父です。
sodesu. soshite kore wa watashi no chichi desu

That's right. And this is my father.

子供さんはいますか?
kodomo san wa imasuka

Do you have any children?

Conversational tip Forming a question in Japanese is straightforward. Generally, you add the question marker か *ka* to the end of a sentence: *a-re wa musuko san desu* (*That's your son*); *a-re wa musuko san desuka* (*Is that your son?*). In less formal spoken Japanese, the question marker is sometimes dropped: *a-re wa musuko san*.

4 Useful phrases (3 minutes)

Read these phrases aloud several times and try to memorize them. Conceal the Japanese with the cover flap and test yourself.

Do you have any siblings? (formal)	ご兄弟はいらっしゃいますか? *go kyohdai wa irasshai masuka*
Do you have any siblings? (informal)	兄弟いる? *kyohdai iru*
Is this your father?	これはお父さんですか? *kore wa otohsan desuka*
Is that your son? (formal)	あれは息子さんですか? *a-re wa musuko san desuka*
This is Akiko's daughter.	これは明子さんの娘さんです。 *kore wa Akiko-san no musume san desu*
Is that your little sister? (informal)	あれは妹? *a-re wa imohto*

いいえ、でも妹がいます。
ihe, demo imohto ga imasu

No, but I have a little sister.

5 Say it (2 minutes)

Is this your wife?

Is that your little brother?

Do you have a son? (informal)

This is Akiko's mother.

1 Warm up (1 minute)

Say "See you tomorrow."
(pp.8-9)

Say "I'm married"
(pp.10-11) and
"Is this your wife?"
(pp.12-13)

DESU/GA ARIMASU
To be/there is

The most common verb in Japanese is *desu*, meaning *is*, *are*, or *am*. The u is pronounced only slightly, often making it sound more like *dess*. *Desu* is placed at the end of a sentence and does not change depending on the subject (*I, you, he,* etc.): *watashi wa Robahto desu* (*I'm Robert*).

2 Useful phrases with desu (2 minutes)

Notice that you'll often find the marker は *wa* or が *ga* after the subject of a sentence. The word order is: subject + *wa/ga* (subject marker) + rest of sentence + *desu*.

私は日本人です。 *watashi wa nihonjin desu*	I'm Japanese.
今10時です。 *ima jyuji desu*	It's ten o'clock.
あなたはお医者 さんですか? *anata wa oisha san desuka*	Are you a doctor?
明子さんは学生です。 *Akiko-san wa gakusei desu*	Akiko is a student.

Read it It's not as difficult to decipher Japanese script as it may at first appear. The most important thing to appreciate initially is that typical Japanese sentences consist of a mixture of three different character systems:

1. *Kanji:* Traditional Chinese characters imported into Japanese, e.g. 車 *kuruma* (car), 母 *haha* (my mother). *Kanji* represent an idea, rather than a particular sound.

2. *Hiragana:* Japanese characters representing syllables, e.g. で *de,* れ *re. Hiragana* is often used for grammatical words such as です *desu* (is), あれ *a-re* (that).

3. *Katakana:* A second syllabary mainly used for foreign loan words, e.g. アメリカ *amerika* (America), ケーキ *kehki* (cake).

私はイギリス人です。
watashi wa igirisu jin desu
I'm British.

3 Useful phrases: talking about what you have (5 minutes)

An informal and straightforward way to talk about what you have is to use the expression (*ga/wa*) *arimasu*, literally meaning *there is*. This changes to (*ga/wa*) *imasu* when talking about people rather than objects.

I have three children.	子供が三人います。 *kodomo ga san nin imasu*
My son has a car.	息子には車が あります。 *musuko niwa kuruma ga arimasu*
I have a little sister.	妹がいます。 *imohto ga imasu*
Do you have any children?	子供さんはいますか? *kodomo san wa imasuka*

名刺があります。
meishi ga arimasu
I have a business card.

4 Negatives (3 minutes)

Negative sentences are made in different ways in Japanese but sometimes use the negative phrase *arimasen*. Learn these phrases and then test yourself by concealing the answers with the cover flap.

We're not American.	アメリカ人ではありません。 *amerika jin dewa arimasen*
I don't have a car.	車がありません。 *kuruma ga arimasen*

5 Put into practice (4 minutes)

Join in this conversation. Read the Japanese beside the pictures on the left and then follow the instructions to make your reply. Then test yourself by concealing the answers with the cover flap.

こんばんは。 *konbanwa* Good evening. Say: Good evening. I'm Robert.	こんばんは。私は ロバートです。 *konbanwa. watashi wa Robahto desu*
どうぞよろしく。 *dohzo yoroshiku* Pleased to meet you. Say: I have a business card.	名刺があります。 *meishi ga arimasu*

FUKUSHU TO KURIKAESH
Review and repeat

Kotae
Answers (Cover with flap)

1 How many?

❶ 三
san

❷ 九
kyu

❸ 四
shi/yon

❹ 二
ni

❺ 八
hachi

❻ 十
jyu

❼ 五
go

❽ 七
shichi/nana

❾ 六
roku

1 How many? (2 minutes)

Hide the answers with the cover flap. Then say these Japanese numbers aloud. Check you have remembered the Japanese correctly.

3 ❶
9 ❷
4 ❸
2 ❹
8 ❺
10 ❻
5 ❼
7 ❽
6 ❾

2 Hello

❶ こんばんは。
私の名前は...です。
konbanwa. watashi no namae wa...desu

❷ どうぞ、よろしく。
dohzo yoroshiku

❸ 息子が二人います。
子供さんはいます
か?
musuko ga futari imasu. kodomo san wa imasuka

❹ さようなら。
sayohnara

2 Hello (4 minutes)

You meet someone in a formal situation. Join in the conversation, replying in Japanese following the English prompts.

konbanwa. watashi no namae wa Maeda Mikiro desu
❶ Answer the greeting and give your name.

kore wa watashi no tsuma desu
❷ Say "Pleased to meet you."

kodomo san wa imasuka
❸ Say "I have two sons. Do you have any children?"

kodomo ga yo nin imasu
❹ Say "Goodbye" formally.

3 Be or have (5 minutes)

Fill in the blanks with *desu* (to be) or *arimasu/imasu* (there is/are used to mean *has/have*). Then check you have remembered correctly.

❶ *watashi wa nihonjin* _____

❷ *ani ga* _____

❸ *anata wa gakusei san* _____ *ka*

❹ *Sarah-san wa igirisu jin* _____

❺ *watashi no namae wa Okada* _____

❻ *meishi ga* _____

❼ *kore wa watashi no otto* _____

❽ *musume ga futari* _____

3 Be or have

❶ です
   desu

❷ います
   imasu

❸ です
   desu

❹ です
   desu

❺ です
   desu

❻ あります
   arimasu

❼ です
   desu

❽ います
   imasu

4 Family (4 minutes)

Say the Japanese for each of the numbered family members. Check you have remembered the Japanese correctly.

❶ my grandmother
❷ my grandfather
❸ my father
my daughter ❻
❺ my son
❹ my mother

4 Family

❶ 祖母
   sobo

❷ 祖父
   sofu

❸ 父
   chichi

❹ 母
   haha

❺ 息子
   musuko

❻ 娘
   musume

Warm up (1 minute)

Count up to ten.
(pp.10-11)

Remind yourself how
to say "hello" and
"goodbye." (pp.8-9)

Ask "Do you have
any children?" (pp.14-15)

KAFE DE
In the café

You will find different types of cafés in
Japan: there are traditional cafés, the
most common of which is called **an-mitsu
kissa**; and Western-style coffee houses,
simply called **kafe** or **kissaten**. These
cafés are very popular, particularly
among younger Japanese.

Words to remember (5 minutes)

Look at the words below and say them out aloud a
few times. Conceal the Japanese with the cover flap
and try to remember each one in turn. Practice the
words on the right as well.

ココア *kokoah*	hot chocolate
ミルクティー *miruku tih*	tea with milk
お茶 *ocha*	(green) tea
サンドイッチ *sando icchi*	sandwich

紅茶
kohcha
(red) tea

Cultural tip The generic Japanese word for tea is *cha*.
In a regular café, Japanese *green tea* would be called *ocha*,
sencha, or *ryokucha*. Western-style tea is known as
kohcha (*red tea*).

In conversation (4 minutes)

コーヒーをお願い
します。
koh-hi o onegai shimasu

A coffee, please.

他にご注文は?
hoka ni gochumon wa

Anything else?

ケーキはありますか?
kehki wa arimasuka

Do you have any cakes?

4 Useful phrases (5 minutes)

Learn these phrases. Read the English under the
pictures and say the phrase in Japanese as shown
on the right. Then cover up the answers on the
right and test yourself.

ケーキ
kehki
cake

A coffee, please.

コーヒーをお願い
します。
koh-hi o onegai shimasu

Anything else?

他にご注文は?
hoka ni gochumon wa

砂糖
satoh
sugar

A cake, too, please.

ケーキもお願いします。
kehki mo onegai shimasu

How much is that?

いくらですか?
ikura desuka

コーヒー
koh-hi
coffee

はい、ございます。
hai, gozaimasu

Yes, certainly.

じゃケーキをお願い
します。いくらですか?
*jya kehki o onegai shimasu.
ikura desuka*

Then I'd like a cake. How
much is that?

800円です。
happyaku yen desu

That's 800 yen.

RESUTORAN DE
In the restaurant

Warm up (1 minute)

Say "A coffee, please."
(pp.18-19)

Say "I don't have a car."
(pp.14-15)

Ask "Do you have any
cakes?" (pp.18-19)

There are different types of eating places in Japan.
In a bar or café, you can find snacks or a light meal.
A *ryohteh* serves traditional Japanese food.
Department stores often house relaxed *resutoran*
on the upper floors, open until about 10 p.m. and
serving both international and Japanese dishes.

Words to remember (3 minutes)

Familiarize yourself with these words
and test yourself using the flap.

メニュー *menyu*	menu
ワインリスト *wain risuto*	wine list
スターター *stahtah*	appetizers
メインコース *mein kohsu*	entrées
デザート *dezahto*	desserts
朝食 *chohshoku*	breakfast
昼食 *chu-shoku*	lunch
夕食 *yu-shoku*	dinner

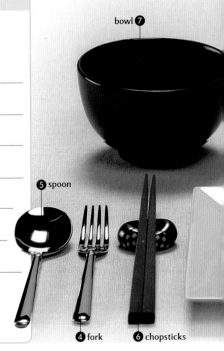

bowl ❼

❺ spoon

❹ fork ❻ chopsticks

In conversation (4 minutes)

四人用のテーブルは空いて
いますか?
*yonin yoh no tehburu wa
aite imasuka*

Do you have a table
for four?

予約なさっていますか?
yoyaku nasatte imasuka

Do you have a
reservation?

はい。バーカーで
予約しています。
*hai. Barker de yoyaku
shite imasu*

Yes, in the name
of Barker.

4 Match and repeat (5 minutes)

Look at the numbered items in this table setting and match them with the Japanese words on the right. Read the Japanese words aloud. Now, conceal the Japanese with the cover flap and test yourself.

❶ glass

napkin ❷

plate ❸

❶ グラス
gurasu

❷ おしぼり
oshibori

❸ 皿
sara

❹ フォーク
fohku

❺ スプーン
supuun

❻ おはし
ohashi

❼ ボール
bohru

5 Useful phrases (2 minutes)

Practice these phrases and then test yourself using the cover flap to conceal the Japanese.

What type of sushi do you have?	どんな種類の寿司がありますか? *don-na shurui no sushi ga arimasuka*
Where can I pay?	どこで払えますか? *doko de harae masuka*

席はどこがよろしいですか?
seki wa doko ga yoroshii desuka

Where would you like to sit?

窓際の席をお願いします。
madogiwa no seki o onegai shimasu

Near a window, please.

はい。こちらへどうぞ。
hai. kochira e dohzo

Very well. Here you are.

TABEMONO
Dishes

A typical meal in Japan would consist of rice and miso soup, together with a variety of fish, meat, and vegetable dishes. The meal is served with pickles and other condiments, such as ginger and horseradish. Dessert is usually a selection of fruit. Sweet desserts are not very common.

1 Warm up (1 minute)

Say "I'm married" (pp.10-11) and "I'm British." (pp.14-15)

Ask "Do you have any siblings?" (pp.12-13)

Say "A sandwich, please." (pp.18-19)

Cultural tip In restaurants and food courts, *tehshoku* (*set menus*) are popular, particularly at lunchtime. These consist of a soup, rice, pickles, and other dishes of your choice—all presented on a tray.

2 Match and repeat (4 minutes)

Look at the numbered items and match them to the Japanese words in the panel on the left.

❶ 果物
kudamono

❷ きのこ
kinoko

❸ 米
kome

❹ 野菜
yasai

❺ スープ
supu

❻ 麺類
men rui

❼ 魚
sakana

❽ 肉
niku

❾ シーフード
shifudo

fruit ❶

❷ mushrooms

rice ❸

❺ soup

fish ❼

❽ meat

3 Words to remember: cooking methods (3 minutes)

Familiarize yourself with
these words.

fried	揚げた
	ageta
grilled	焼いた
	yaita
roasted	ロ一ストした
	rohsuto shita
boiled	ゆでた
	yudeta
steamed	蒸した
	mushita
raw	生の
	nama no

この魚は生のですか？
*kono sakana wa nama
no desuka*
Is this fish raw?

4 Say it (2 minutes)

What's *Yakitori*?

A beer, please.

Is this fish grilled?

tables ④

5 Words to remember: drinks (3 minutes)

Familiarize yourself with these words.

water	水
	mizu
mineral water	ミネラルウォ一タ一
	mineraru wohtah
sake	お酒
	osake
wine	ワイン
	wain
beer	ビ一ル
	bihru
fruit juice	フル一ツジュ一ス
	furutsu jyusu

noodles ⑥

6 Useful phrases (2 minutes)

Practice these phrases and then test yourself.

I'm vegetarian.	ベジタリアンです。
	bejitarian desu
I'm allergic to nuts.	ナッツ類でアレルギ一反応を起こします。
	nattsu rui de arerugih hannoh o okoshimasu
What's Chirinabe?	ちり鍋とは何ですか？
	chirinabe towa nan desuka

⑨ seafood

SHITE KUDASAI
Requests

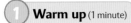

1 Warm up (1 minute)

What are "breakfast," "lunch," and "dinner" in Japanese? (pp.20–21)

Say "I'm vegetarian" and "What's Sukiyaki?" in Japanese. (pp.22–23)

The simplest way to ask for something in Japanese is to say what you want, followed by *o–onegai shimasu* (*please*). You can use this in almost any situation. However, if you really want to impress—for example, in a business situation—you could use the polite formula *itadake masuka*.

2 Basic requests (6 minutes)

Here are some phrases using *(o) onegai shimasu* for making basic requests in Japanese. Learn these phrases and then test yourself by using the cover flap.

紅茶をお願いします。 *kohcha o onegai shimasu*	(I'd like) some tea, please.
ケーキをお願いします。 *kehki o onegai shimasu*	(I'd like) a cake, please.
フォークをお願いします。 *fohku o onegai shimasu*	(I'd like) a fork, please.
3人用のテーブル をお願いします。 *san nin yoh no tehburu o onegai shimasu*	(I'd like) a table for three, please.
メニューをお願いします。 *menyu o onegai shimasu*	(I'd like) the menu, please.
キャンディをお願いします。 *kyandih o onegai shimasu*	(I'd like) some candy, please.
満タンでお願いします。 *mantan de onegai shimasu*	Fill it up, please. (A full tank, please.)

大和さんおねがい
します。
Yamato-san onegai shimasu
(I'd like) Mr. Yamato, please.

Read it Japanese *kanji* ideograms came from Chinese and are still used today. Some *kanji* are simple and resemble the item they describe, like the character for people: 人 (*jin/nin*), but many are quite intricate. The restaurant sign to the left is written in *kanji*. The three vertical characters say *jyun bi chu* (*preparation in progress*)—a polite way of saying *closed!*

3 Polite requests (4 minutes)

In a business situation, you may want to appear ultra-polite, especially if you're talking to someone senior to yourself. Learn these phrases and then test yourself by using the cover flap.

Would you please help me?	手伝っていただけますか? *tetsudatte itadake masuka*
Could I have your signature here, please?	ここにサインをいただけますか? *koko ni sain o itadake masuka*
Could I have your phone number, please?	電話番号を教えていただけますか? *denwa bangoh o oshiete itadake masuka*

4 Put into practice (4 minutes)

Join in this conversation. Read the Japanese beside the pictures on the left and then follow the instructions to make your reply in Japanese. Test yourself by hiding the answers with the cover flap.

こんばんは。予約なさっていますか?
konbanwa. yoyaku nasatte imasuka

Good evening. Do you have a reservation?

Say: No, but I'd like a table for three.

いいえ、でも3人用のテーブルをお願いします。
ihe, demo san nin yoh no tehburu o onegai shimasu

お飲物は何になさいますか?
onomimono wa nani ni nasai masuka

What would you like to drink?

Say: A beer, please.

ビールをお願いします。
bihru o onegai shimasu

Kotae
Answers (Cover with flap)

FUKUSHU TO KURIKAESH
Review and repeat

1 What food?

❶ スープ
supu
❷ 野菜
yasai
❸ 魚
sakana
❹ 肉
niku
❺ グラス
gurasu
❻ 米
kome

1 What food? (4 minutes)

Name the numbered items.

❶ soup
❷ vegetables
❸ fish
meat ❹
glass ❺

2 This is my ...

❶ これは私の夫
です。
*kore wa watashi no
otto desu*
❷ これは私の娘
です。
*kore wa watashi no
musume desu*
❸ これは私の兄弟
です。
*kore wa watashi no
kyohdai desu*

2 This is my ... (4 minutes)

Say these phrases in
Japanese.

❶ This is my husband.

❷ This is my daughter.

❸ These are my
siblings.

3 I'd like ...

❶ ケーキをお願いします。
*kehki o onegai
shimasu*
❷ 砂糖をお願いします。
*satoh o onegai
shimasu*
❸ コーヒーをお願い
します。
*koh-hi o onegai
shimasu*
❹ 紅茶をお願いします。
*kohcha o onegai
shimasu*

3 I'd like ... (3 minutes)

Say "I'd like" the following:

❹ tea
cake ❶
sugar ❷
coffee ❸

Kotae
Answers (Cover with flap)

rice **6**

chopsticks **7**

8 noodles

10 beer

napkin **9**

1 What food?

7 おはし
ohashi

8 麺類
men rui

9 おしぼり
oshibori

10 ビール
bihru

4 Restaurant (4 minutes)

You arrive at a restaurant. Join in the conversation, replying in Japanese where you see the English prompts.

konbanwa
1 Do you have a table for three?

yoyaku nasatte imasuka
2 Yes, in the name of Barker.

seki wa doko ga yoroshii desuka
3 Near a window, please.

kochira no hoh e dohzo
4 The menu, please.

mochiron gozaimasu
5 Do you have a wine list?

4 Restaurant

1 3人用のテーブルは
空いていますか?
*san nin yoh no tehburu
wa aite imasuka*

2 はい。バーカーで
予約しています。
*hai. Barker de yoyaku
shite imasu*

3 窓際の席をお願いし
ます。
*madogiwa no seki o
onegai shimasu*

4 メニューをお願い
します。
*menyu o onegai
shimasu*

5 ワインリストは
ありますか?
*wain risuto wa
arimasuka*

1 Warm up (1 minute)

How do you say "I have four children"? (pp.10-11)

Now say "We're not British" and "I don't have a car." (pp.14-15)

What is Japanese for "my mother"? (pp.10-11)

HIZUKE TO TOSHITSUKI
Days and months

The most important holiday of the year in Japan is the three-day New Year Holiday (*shohgatsu sanganichi*). The Japanese usually spend this with family. Christmas is also celebrated, but more often spent with friends.

2 Words to remember: days of the week (5 minutes)

Familiarize yourself with these words and test yourself using the flap.

月曜日 *getsuyoh bi*	Monday
火曜日 *kayoh bi*	Tuesday
水曜日 *suiyoh bi*	Wednesday
木曜日 *mokuyoh bi*	Thursday
金曜日 *kin-yoh bi*	Friday
土曜日 *doyoh bi*	Saturday
日曜日 *nichiyoh bi*	Sunday
今日 *kyoh*	today
明日 *ashita*	tomorrow
昨日 *kinoh*	yesterday

明日お会いしましょう。
ashita oai shimashoh
We meet tomorrow.

今日予約があります。
kyoh yoyaku ga arimasu
I have a reservation for today.

3 Useful phrases: days (2 minutes)

Learn these phrases and then test yourself using the cover flap.

ミーティングは火曜日ではありません。 *mihtingu wa kayoh bi dewa arimasen*	The meeting isn't on Tuesday.
日曜日に仕事をします。 *nichiyoh bi ni shigoto o shimasu*	I work on Sundays.

4 Words to remember: months of the year (5 minutes)

Japanese months are named simply
1 month, 2 month, etc.

私たちの記念日は七月です。
watashi tachi no kinenbi
wa shichi gatsu desu
Our anniversary is in July.

January	一月	*ichi gatsu*
February	二月	*ni gatsu*
March	三月	*san gatsu*
April	四月	*shi gatsu*
May	五月	*go gatsu*
June	六月	*roku gatsu*
July	七月	*shichi gatsu*
August	八月	*hachi gatsu*
September	九月	*ku gatsu*
October	十月	*jyu gatsu*
November	十一月	*jyu-ichi gatsu*
December	十二月	*jyu-ni gatsu*
next month	来月	*rai getsu*
last month	先月	*sen getsu*

クリスマスは十二月です。
kurisumasu wa jyu-ni
gatsu desu
Christmas is in December.

5 Useful phrases: months (2 minutes)

Learn these phrases and then test yourself using
the cover flap.

My children are on vacation in August.	子供たちは八月は休みです。 *kodomo tachi wa hachi gatsu wa yasumi desu*
My birthday is in June.	私の誕生日は六月です。 *watashi no tanjyoh bi wa roku gatsu desu*

JIKAN TO SUHJI
Time and numbers

When telling the time in Japanese, the hour comes first—for example, *ichi ji* (*one o'clock*), *ni ji* (*two o'clock*), etc., followed by the minutes: *go fun* (*five minutes*), *jippun* (*ten minutes*). *Mae* is added for times before the hour: *ni ji nippun mae* (*ten to two*, literally *two o'clock ten minutes before*).

2 Words to remember: time (4 minutes)

Memorize how to tell the time in Japanese.

1時 *ichi ji*	one o'clock
1時5分 *ichi ji go fun*	five past one
1時15分 *ichi ji jyu-go fun*	quarter past one
1時20分 *ichi ji nijyuppun*	twenty past one
1時半 *ichi ji han*	half past one
1時45分 *ichi ji yonjyu-go fun*	quarter to two ("one forty-five")
2時10分前 *ni ji jippun mae*	ten to two

3 Useful phrases (2 minutes)

Learn these phrases and then test yourself using the cover flap.

今何時ですか? *ima nanji desuka*	What time is it?
朝食は何時がいい ですか? *chohshoku wa nanji ga iidesuka*	At what time do you want breakfast?
12時に予約を 入れています。 *jyu-ni ji ni yoyaku o ireteimasu*	I have a reservation for twelve o'clock.

4 Words to remember: higher numbers (6 minutes)

Japanese numbers are very logical. To count above ten, the individual numbers are simply added together. So 11 is *jyu-ichi* (ten-one), 15 is *jyu-go* (ten-five), etc. Be careful, though, to put the numbers in the right order: *go-jyu* is 50 (five-ten), *nana-jyu* is 70 (seven-ten). Units are added directly after the tens: 68 is *roku-jyu hachi*; 25 is *ni-jyu go*, and so on.

Pay special attention to the number 10,000, which is *man* or *ichi-man*. A million is *hyaku-man* (one hundred-ten thousands).

五千円です。
go-sen yen desu
That's 5,000 yen.

eleven	十一	*jyu-ichi*
twelve	十二	*jyu-ni*
thirteen	十三	*jyu-san*
fourteen	十四	*jyu-shi/jyu-yon*
fifteen	十五	*jyu-go*
sixteen	十六	*jyu-roku*
seventeen	十七	*jyu-shichi*
eighteen	十八	*jyu-hachi*
nineteen	十九	*jyu-kyu*
twenty	二十	*ni-jyu*
thirty	三十	*san-jyu*
forty	四十	*yon-jyu*
fifty	五十	*go-jyu*
sixty	六十	*roku-jyu*
seventy	七十	*nana-jyu*
eighty	八十	*hachi-jyu*
ninety	九十	*kyu-jyu*
hundred	百	*hyaku*
three hundred	三百	*san-byaku*
one thousand	千	*sen*
ten thousand	一万	*ichi-man*
two hundred thousand	二十万	*ni-jyu-man*
one million	百万	*hyaku-man*

5 Say it (2 minutes)

twenty-five

ninety-two

two hundred

twenty thousand

five to ten

half past eleven

That's 700 yen.

APO/(GO)YOYAKU
Appointments

1 **Warm up** (1 minute)

Say the days of the week.
(pp.28-29)

Say "three o'clock."
(pp.30-31)

What's the Japanese for
"today," "tomorrow," and
"yesterday"? (pp.28-29)

The Japanese are eager to find out about the status
of someone they meet for the first time. This is in
order to judge the level of respect due and appropriate
formality of the language. The most common way
of establishing status is by the virtually obligatory
exchange of *business cards* (**meishi**).

2 **Useful phrases** (5 minutes)

Learn these phrases and then test yourself.

明日お会い しましょうか? *ashita oai shimashohka*	Shall we meet tomorrow?
どなたとですか? *donata to desuka*	With whom? (formal)
いつお暇ですか? *itsu ohima desuka*	When are you free?
すみません。 その日は忙しいです。 *sumimasen. sonohi wa isogashih desu*	Sorry. I'm busy that day.
木曜日はどうですか? *mokuyoh bi wa doh desuka*	How about Thursday?
大丈夫です。 *daijyohbu desu*	That's good for me.

ようこそ。
yohkoso
Welcome.

3 **In conversation** (4 minutes)

こんにちは。アポを入れて
いるのですが。
*konnichiwa. apo o
ireteiru no desuga*

Hello. I have
an appointment.

どなたとですか?
donata to desuka

With whom?

田中さんとです。
Tanaka-san to desu

With Mr. Tanaka.

4 Put into practice (5 minutes)

Practice these phrases. Then cover up the text on the right and say the answering part of the dialogue in Japanese. Check your answers and repeat if necessary.

木曜日にお会いしましょうか？
mokuyoh bi ni oai shimashohka

Shall we meet on Thursday?

Say: Sorry. I'm busy that day.

すみません。
その日は忙しいです。
sumimasen. sonohi wa isogashih desu

いつお暇ですか？
itsu ohima desuka

When are you free?

Say: On Tuesday in the afternoon.

火曜日の午後なら空いています。
kayoh bi no gogo nara aite imasu

私も大丈夫です。
watashi mo daijyohbu desu

That's good for me, too.

Ask: At what time?

何時がよろしいですか？
nanji ga yoroshih desuka

Read it It's useful to recognize some common Japanese signs you might see around a building. The signs below are a combination of two *kanji* characters. *Madoguchi* means literally *window mouth*!

 uketsuke
(reception)

 madoguchi
(information desk)

そうですか。
何時のご予約ですか？
sohdesuka. nanji no goyoyaku desuka

Very good. What time is the appointment?

3時ですが。
san ji desuga

At three o'clock.

どうぞ、おかけください。
dohzo okake kudasai

Take a seat, please.

DENWA DE
On the telephone

1 **Warm up** (1 minute)

How do you say "sorry"? (pp.32-33)

Ask "Shall we meet tomorrow?" (pp.32-33)

Say "(I'd like) a cake, please." (pp.24-25)

The Japanese answer the telephone with *moshi moshi* (hello), rather than *konnichiwa*. If you will be using your own cellphone in Japan, note that you can use it for data only (using roaming, or a local SIM card). In order to make calls to Japanese numbers, you will need to rent a Japanese phone.

2 **Match and repeat** (6 minutes)

Match the numbered items to the Japanese in the panel below and test yourself.

❶ チャージャー
chahjyah

❷ 留守番電話
rusuban denwa

❸ 電話
denwa

❹ SIMカード
simu cahdo

❺ 携帯
kehtai

❻ イヤフォン
iyafon

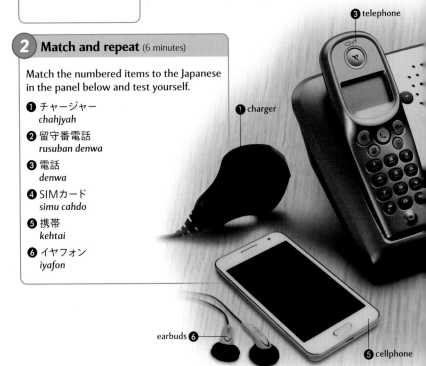

❸ telephone
❶ charger
earbuds **❻**
❺ cellphone

3 **In conversation** (4 minutes)

もしもし、ジャパニーズ コネクションです。
moshi moshi, japanihzu konekushon desu

Hello. This is Japanese Connection.

もしもし、
岡田さんをお願いします。
moshi moshi, Okada-san o onegai shimasu

Hello. (I'd like to speak to) Ms. Okada, please.

どちら様ですか?
dochira sama desuka

Who's speaking?

4 SIM card

SIMカードをください。
simu cahdo o kudasai
I want to buy a SIM card,
please.

2 answering machine

4 Useful phrases (4 minutes)

Practice these phrases. Then test yourself using the cover flap.

ゴープレス・プリンターの番号を教えてください。
Gopress purintah no bangoh o oshiete kudasai

I'd like the number for Gopress Printers.

岡田さんをお願いします。
Okada-san o onegai shimasu

(I'd like to speak to) Mr./Ms. Okada, please.

メッセージを伝えていただけますか？
messehji o tsutaete itadake masuka

Can I leave a message?

すみません、
番号を間違えました。
sumimasen, bangoh o machigae mashita

Sorry, I have the wrong number.

ゴープレス・プリンターの前田美樹朗と申します。
Gopress purintah no Maeda Mikiro to mohshimasu

Maeda Mikiro of Gopress Printers.

すみません。ただ今話し中です。
sumimasen. tadaima hanashichu desu

I'm sorry. The line is busy.

岡田さんの方から連絡いただけますか？
Okada-san no hokara renraku itadake masuka

Can Ms. Okada call me back, please?

FUKUSHU TO KURIKAESHI
Review and repeat

1 Sums

❶ 十六
  jyu-roku

❷ 三十九
  san-jyu kyu

❸ 五十三
  go-jyu san

❹ 七十八
  nana-jyu hachi

❺ 九十九
  kyu-jyu kyu

❻ 十七
  jyu-shichi

1 Sums (4 minutes)

Say the answers to these sums out loud in Japanese. Then check you have remembered correctly.

❶ 10 + 6 = ?
❷ 14 + 25 = ?
❸ 66 − 13 = ?
❹ 40 + 38 = ?
❺ 90 + 9 = ?
❻ 20 − 3 = ?

3 Telephones (3 minutes)

What are the numbered items in Japanese?

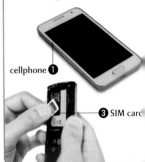

cellphone ❶

❸ SIM card

2 To want

❶ します
  shimasu

❷ お願い
  onegai

❸ ますか
  masuka

❹ いただけ
  itadake

❺ お願い
  onegai

❻ 人
  nin

2 To want (3 minutes)

Fill the blanks in the requests with the correct word.

❶ *Yamato-san onegai _____ .*

❷ *kyandih o _____ shimasu.*

❸ *koko ni sain o itadake _____ .*

❹ *tetsudatte _____ masuka.*

❺ *bihru o _____ shimasu.*

❻ *san _____ yoh no tehburu o onegai shimasu.*

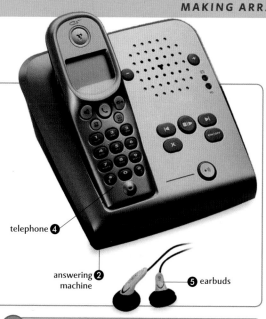

telephone **4**

answering **2**
machine

5 earbuds

Kotae
Answers (Cover with flap)

3 Telephones

❶ 携帯
kehtai

❷ 留守番電話
rusuban denwa

❸ SIMカード
simu cardo

❹ 電話
denwa

❺ イヤフォン
iyafon

---

4 When? (2 minutes)

What do these sentences mean?

❶ *dewa mata ashita*

❷ *doyoh bi ni shigoto o shimasu*

❸ *watashi no tanjyoh bi wa go gatsu desu*

❹ *kyoh yoyaku ga arimasu*

4 When?

❶ See you tomorrow.

❷ I work on Saturday.

❸ My birthday is in May.

❹ I have a reservation for today.

---

5 Time (3 minutes)

Say these times in Japanese.

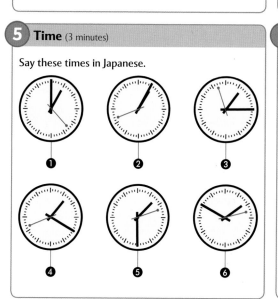

5 Time

❶ 1時
ichi ji

❷ 1時5分
ichi ji go fun

❸ 1時15分
ichi ji jyu-go fun

❹ 1時20分
ichi ji nijyuppun

❺ 1時半
ichi ji han

❻ 2時10分前
ni ji jippun mae

1 **Warm up** (1 minute)

Count to 100 in tens.
(pp.10-11 and pp.30-31)

Ask "What time is it?"
(pp.30-31)

Say "half past one."
(pp.30-31)

EKI DE
At the station

Japan is famous for its clean, fast, and reliable train services. The network covers the entire country, and there are different types of trains: local *futsu* and *kaisoku* commuter trains, *kyuko* and *tokkyu* express trains; and the famous *shinkansen* high-speed intercity "bullet" trains.

2 **Words to remember** (3 minutes)

Learn these words and then test yourself.

駅 *eki*	station
電車 *densha*	train
プラットホーム *purattohohmu*	platform
チケット *chiketto*	ticket
片道 *katamichi*	one-way
往復 *ohfuku*	round-trip
一等 / 二等車 *ittoh/nitoh sha*	first/second class
乗り換え *norikae*	change (trains)

改札口 *kaisatsu guchi* ticket barrier

サイン *sain* sign

乗客 *jyohkyaku* passenger

この駅は混んでいます。
kono eki wa konde imasu
This station is crowded.

3 **In conversation** (4 minutes)

京都行きを二枚おねがいします。
Kyoto iki o nimai onegai shimasu

Two to Kyoto, please.

往復ですか?
ohfuku desuka

Is that round-trip?

はい。席の予約が必要ですか?
hai. seki no yoyaku ga hitsuyo desuka

Yes. Do I need to make seat reservations?

4 Useful phrases (5 minutes)

大阪への電車は遅れて
います。
*Osaka eno densha wa
okurete imasu*
The train for Osaka is late.

Learn these phrases and then test yourself using
the cover flap.

How much is a ticket to Nagasaki?	長崎行きのチケット はいくらですか? *Nagasaki iki no chiketto wa ikura desuka*
Can I use a credit card?	クレジットカード が使えますか? *kurejitto kahdo ga tsukae masuka*
Do I have to change?	乗り換えしなければ いけませんか? *norikae shinakereba ikemasenka*
Which platform does the train leave from?	電車はどのプラットホーム から発車しますか? *densha wa dono purattohohmu kara hassha shimasuka*
What time does the train leave?	電車は何時に発車しますか? *densha wa nanji ni hassha shimasuka*

5 Say it (2 minutes)

This train is crowded.

How much is a ticket to Osaka?

Cultural tip You might need to buy your train tickets from machines. These machines can be complicated to navigate, and you may need someone to help you. But all the destinations are written in phonetic *katakana* characters, as well as *kanji*, to help children (and foreigners) to read the signs.

いいえ。一万円に
なります。
*ihe. ichiman-yen
ni narimasu*

No. That's 10,000 yen.

クレジットカード
が使えますか?
*kurejitto kahdo ga
tsukae masuka*

Can I use a credit card?

はい。電車はプラット
ホーム1番から発車します。
*hai. densha wa
purattohohmu ichiban
kara hassha shimasu*

Yes. The train leaves
from platform one.

1 Warm up (1 minute)

How do you say "train"? (pp.38–39)

What are "tomorrow" and "yesterday" in Japanese? (pp.28–29)

Count from 10 to 20. (pp.30–31)

IKU/NORU
To go and to take

Iku (*to go*) and *noru* (*to take*) are essential verbs you will need as you find your way around. Japanese verbs do not change according to the subject, but do have different endings for the tense (present/past) or mood (requesting/wanting, etc.). Note also that the verb usually comes at the end of a sentence.

2 Iku/noru: to go and to take (6 minutes)

The basic verb (*iku/noru*) can be used by itself, but often an ending is added. The present tense of Japanese verbs generally ends in *-masu*: *ikimasu* (*go, am/are/is going*) and the negative in *-masen*: *ikemasen* (*don't go, am not/aren't/isn't going*). The "wanting" mood ends in *-tai*: *noritai* (*want to take*).

どこ行くの？ *doko iku no*	Where are you going? (informal)
どこに行かれるの ですか？ *doko ni ikareru no desuka*	Where are you going? (formal)
今日は自転車に 乗ります。 *kyoh wa jitensha ni norimasu*	I'm taking my bicycle today.
バスで仕事に 行きます。 *basu de shigoto ni ikimasu*	I go to work by bus.
タクシーでは仕事に 行きません。 *takushih dewa shigotoni ikimasen*	I don't go to work by taxi.
電車に乗りたい です。 *densha ni noritai desu*	I want to take the train.

富士山に行きます。
fujisan ni ikimasu
I'm going to Mount Fuji.

Cultural tip Taxis in Japan are often yellow or green. There's usually a light at the bottom right of the windshield: green for occupied and red for available. The taxis are usually scrupulously clean—drivers even wear white gloves. Back doors are remote-controlled by the driver, so be careful you don't get knocked over as you reach for the handle. Tips are not usual.

3 Past and future (6 minutes)

The ending *-mashita* shows a verb is in the past: *norimashita* (took), *ikimashita* (went). There is no special form for the future. Instead, the present tense can be used with a time indicator, e.g. *ashita* (tomorrow).

タクシーに乗りました。
takushih ni norimashita

I took a taxi.

富士山に電車で行きました。
fujisan ni densha de ikimashita

I went to Mount Fuji by train.

明日地下鉄に乗ります。
ashita chikatetsu ni norimasu

I'll take the subway tomorrow.

明日バスで仕事に行きます。
ashita basu de shigoto ni ikimasu

I'll go to work by bus tomorrow.

4 Put into practice (2 minutes)

Cover the text on the right and complete the dialogue in Japanese.

どこに行かれるのですか?
doko ni ikareru no desuka

駅に行きます。
eki ni ikimasu

Where are you going?

Say: I'm going to the station.

地下鉄に乗りたいですか?
chikatetsu ni noritai desuka

いいえ、バスに乗りたいです。
ihe, basu ni noritai desu

Do you want to take the subway?

Say: No, I want to take the bus.

三十四番のバスですよ。
san-jyu yon ban no basu desuyo

どうもありがとうございます。
dohmo arigatoh gozaimasu

That'll be bus number 34.

Say: Thank you very much.

1 Warm up (1 minute)

Say "I want to go to the station." (pp.40–41)

Ask "Where are you going?" (pp.40–41)

What's 45 in Japanese? (pp.30–31)

TAKUSHIH, BASU, CHIKATETSU
Taxi, bus, and subway

On buses, you generally take a ticket from a machine as you get on. At the end of your journey, a chart will indicate how much you have to pay.

2 Words to remember (4 minutes)

Familiarize yourself with these words.

バス	*basu*	bus
タクシー	*takushih*	taxi
地下鉄	*chikatetsu*	subway
バス停	*basu teh*	bus station
タクシー乗り場	*takushih noriba*	taxi stand
地下鉄の駅	*chikatetsu no eki*	subway station
運賃	*unchin*	fare
線	*sen*	line/route

88番のバスはここで
停まりますか?
*hachijyu-hachi ban no basu
wa kokode tomarimasuka*
Does the number 88
stop here?

3 In conversation: taxi (2 minutes)

秋葉原までお願い
します。
*Akihabara ma-de
onegai shimasu*

To Akihabara, please.

わかりました。
wakarimashita

Very well.

ここで降ろしてください。
kokode oroshite kudasai

Can you drop me
here, please?

4 Useful phrases (4 minutes)

Learn these phrases and then test yourself using the cover flap.

A taxi to Ginza, please.	銀座までのタクシーをお願いします。 *Ginza ma-de no takushih o onegai shimasu*
What time is the next bus to the airport?	空港行きの次のバスは何時ですか? *ku-koh iki no tsugi no basu wa nanji desuka*
How do you get to Asakusa?	浅草にはどうやって行けばいいですか? *Asakusa niwa dohyatte ikeba iidesuka*
Please wait for me.	ちょっと待ってください。 *chotto matte kudasai*

Cultural tip Tokyo, Osaka, and other major cities have extensive and efficient metro systems. The different lines (**sen**) have names such as **yamanote-sen** (*a circular line which links the network*). Fares vary depending on distance.

東京メトロ
Tokyo Metro

5 Say it (2 minutes)

To the station, please.

A taxi to the airport, please.

How do you get to Akihabara?

6 In conversation: bus (2 minutes)

博物館へ行きますか?
hakubutsu kan e ikimasuka

Do you go to the museum?

はい。あまり遠くないですよ。
hai. amari tohku naidesuyo

Yes. It's not very far.

どこでおりるか教えてもらえますか?
doko de oriru ka oshiete mora-e masuka

Can you tell me when to get off?

DOHRO DE
On the road

How do you say "A coffee, please"? (pp.14-15)

Say "my father," "my sister," and "my parents." (pp.12-13)

Say "I'm going to Ginza." (pp.40-41)

Gairaigo is a special term used to refer to the many foreign words imported into Japanese, mainly from English. In some areas of life, such as modern machinery and computers, *gairaigo* is dominant. Pay attention, though, to the particularly Japanese way of pronouncing the words.

2 Match and repeat (4 minutes)

Match the numbered items to the list below, then test yourself.

❶ フロントガラス
furonto garasu

❷ ボンネット
bon-netto

❸ バンパー
banpah

❹ タイヤ
taiya

❺ ヘッドライト
heddo raito

❻ ドア
doa

❼ 車輪
shahrin

❽ トランク
toranku

❾ サイドミラー
saido mirah

Cultural tip Japan is one of the few countries that drives on the left, unlike the US. Many highways are toll roads and can be expensive.

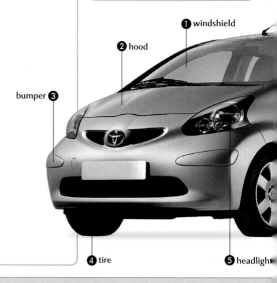

❶ windshield
❷ hood
bumper ❸
❹ tire
❺ headlight

3 Road signs (2 minutes)

一方通行
ippoh tsu-koh

One way

徐行
jyokoh

Proceed slowly

最低速度
saiteh sokudo

Minimum speed limit

4 Useful phrases (4 minutes)

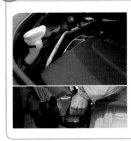

Learn these phrases and then test yourself using the cover flap.

The engine won't start.	エンジンがかかりません。 *enjin ga kakari masen*
Fill it up, please. (A full tank, please.)	満タンお願いします。 *mantan onegai shimasu*

5 Say it (1 minute)

Diesel, please.

The car won't start.

⑨ side mirror

⑧ trunk

⑥ door   **⑦** wheel

6 Words to remember (3 minutes)

Familiarize yourself with these words, then test yourself using the flap.

driver's license	運転免許証 *unten menkyosho*
gasoline	ガソリン *gasorin*
diesel	ディーゼル *dihzeru*
oil	オイル *oiru*
engine	エンジン *enjin*
flat tire	パンク *panku*

Read it Road signs are often in Japanese characters only. If you're driving, familiarize yourself with the Japanese script for your destination, as well as the more common signs, such as 止まれ *tomare* (stop).

止まれ
tomare

Stop

進入禁止
shin-nyu kinshi

No entry

駐車禁止
chu-sha kinshi

No parking

Kotae
Answers (Cover with flap)

FUKUSHU TO KURIKAESHI
Review and repeat

1 Transportation

❶ バス
basu

❷ タクシー
takushih

❸ 車
kuruma

❹ 自転車
jitensha

❺ 地下鉄
chikatetsu

1 Transportation (3 minutes)

Name the transportation type in Japanese.

❶ bus

taxi ❷

2 Go and take

❶ 行きます
ikimasu

❷ 乗りたい
noritai

❸ 行く
iku

❹ 行かれる
ikareru

❺ 乗ります
norimasu

❻ 乗りました
norimashita

2 Go and take (4 minutes)

Use the correct form of the verb in parentheses to fill the blanks.

❶ *fujisan ni _____. (iku)*

❷ *densha ni _____ desu. (noru)*

❸ *doko _____ no. (iku)*

❹ *doko ni _____ no desuka. (iku)*

❺ *ashita chikatetsu ni _____. (noru)*

❻ *kinoh takushih ni _____. (noru)*

3 car

4 bicycle

subway **5**

3 Questions
(4 minutes)

How do you ask these questions in Japanese?

❶ "Do you have any cakes?"

❷ "Do you have any children?"

❸ "What time is it?"

❹ "Do you go to the station?"

❺ "Where are you going?" (informal)

❻ "Can I use a credit card?"

3 Questions

❶ ケーキはあります か?
kehki wa arimasuka

❷ 子供さんはいます か?
kodomo san wa imasuka

❸ 今何時ですか?
ima nanji desuka

❹ 駅へ行きますか?
eki e ikimasuka

❺ どこ行くの?
doko iku no

❻ クレジットカード が使えますか?
kurejitto kahdo ga tsukae masuka

4 Tickets (4 minutes)

You're buying tickets at a train station. Join in the conversation, replying in Japanese following the numbered English prompts.

konnichiwa
❶ Two to Osaka, please.

ohfuku desuka
❷ No. One-way, please.

ichiman-yen ni narimasu
❸ What time does the train leave?

ni ji jippun mae desu
❹ Which platform does the train leave from?

purattohohmu wa ichiban desu
❺ Thank you very much.

4 Tickets

❶ 大阪行きを二枚お願 いします。
Osaka iki o nimai onegai shimasu

❷ いいえ。片道をお願 いします。
ihe. katamichi o onegai shimasu

❸ 電車は何時に発車 しますか?
densha wa nanji ni hassha shimasuka

❹ 電車はどのプラット ホームから発車しま すか?
densha wa dono purattohohmu kara hassha shimasuka

❺ どうもありがとう ございます。
dohmo arigato gozaimasu

1 Warm up (1 minute)

Ask "Do you go to the museum?" (pp.42–43)

What are "station" and "ticket" in Japanese? (pp.38–39)

MACHI DE
Around town

To talk about features or facilities, you can use the phrases *ga/wa arimasu* (*there is/are*) and *ga/wa arimasen* (*there isn't/aren't*). Notice the word order is the opposite to English: *hashi no chikaku ni suimingu pu-ru ga arimasu* = bridge/near to/swimming pool/there is (*There's a swimming pool near the bridge*).

2 Match and repeat (4 minutes)

Match the numbered locations to the words in the panel.

❶ 横断歩道
   ohdan hodoh

❷ 橋
   hashi

❸ デパート
   depahto

❹ 駐車場
   chusha jyo

❺ 噴水
   funsui

❻ 広場
   hiroba

❼ 博物館
   hakubutsu kan

❽ 映画館
   eiga kan

3 Words to remember (4 minutes)

Familiarize yourself with these words and test yourself using the cover flap.

ガソリンスタンド *gasorin sutando*	gas station
観光案内所 *kankoh an-naijyo*	tourist information center
スイミングプール *suimingu pu-ru*	swimming pool
ネットカフェ *netto kafeh*	internet café

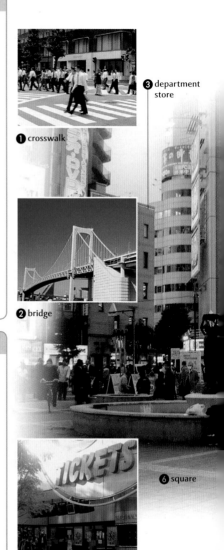

❸ department store

❶ crosswalk

❷ bridge

❻ square

❽ movie theater

4 Useful phrases (4 minutes)

Learn these phrases and then test yourself using the cover flap.

Is there a museum in town?	街に博物館が ありますか？ *machi ni hakubutsu kan ga arimasuka*
Is it far from here?	ここから遠い ですか？ *koko kara toh-i desuka*
There's a swimming pool near the bridge.	橋の近くにスイミング プールがあります。 *hashi no chikaku ni suimingu pu-ru ga arimasu*
There isn't a tourist information center.	観光案内所はありません。 *kankoh an-naijyo wa arimasen*

寺は街の真ん中にあります。
*tera wa machi no man-naka
ni arimasu*
The temple is in the
center of town.

5 Put into practice (2 minutes)

Join in this conversation. Read the Japanese on the left and follow the instructions to make your reply. Then test yourself by concealing the answers with the cover flap.

4 parking lot

5 fountain

どうしました？
doh shimashita

Is everything okay?

Ask: Is there an internet café nearby?

この近くにネットカフェは
ありますか？
*kono chikaku ni netto kafe
wa arimasuka*

いいえ、でも観光案内所
はあります。
*ihe, demo kankoh an-
naijyo wa arimasu*

No, but there's a tourist
information center.

Ask: Is it far from here?

ここから遠い
ですか？
koko kara toh-i desuka

駅の近くです。
eki no chikaku desu

It's near the station.

Say: Thank you.

ありがとうございます。
arigatoh gozaimasu

7 museum

MICHI O KIKU
Asking for directions

1 Warm up (1 minute)

How do you say "bridge" and "fountain"? (pp.48–49)

Ask "Is it far from here?" (pp.48–49)

Ask "Is there a museum in town?" (pp.48–49)

Finding your way around town in Japan can be confusing, so it's a good idea to learn how to ask for and understand directions. Remember that Japanese word order is different from English: **kado o hidari ni magette kudasai** = corner at/left toward/turn/please (*Turn left at the corner*).

2 Useful phrases (4 minutes)

Practice these phrases and then test yourself.

左 / 右に曲がってください。 *hidari/migi ni magatte kudasai*	(Please) turn left/right.
左に / 右に。 *hidari ni/migi ni*	On the left/on the right.
まっすぐに。 *massugu ni*	Straight ahead.
寺にはどうやって行けばいいですか? *tera niwa dohyatte ikeba iidesuka*	How do I get to the temple?
左側の最初の道。 *hidari gawa no saisho no michi*	First street on the left.
右の二番目の道。 *migi no ni-banme no michi*	Second street on the right.

オフィスブロック
ofisu burokku
office block

公園
kohen
park

角を左に曲がってください。
kado o hidari ni magatte kudasai
Turn left at the corner.

3 In conversation (4 minutes)

この街にレストランはありますか?
kono machi ni resutoran wa arimasuka

Is there a restaurant in town?

はい。駅の近くにあります。
hai. eki no chikaku ni arimasu

Yes, near the station.

駅にはどうやって行けばいいですか?
eki niwa dohyatte ikeba iidesuka

How do I get to the station?

4 Words to remember (4 minutes)

道に迷いました。
michi ni mayoi mashita
I'm lost.

Familiarize yourself with these words and test
yourself using the flap.

traffic lights	信号	*shingoh*
corner	角	*kado*
street	道	*michi*
road	道路	*dohro*
map	地図	*chizu*
overpass	立体交差	*rittai kohsa*
across from	反対側	*hantai gawa*
at the end of the street	道の終わりに	*michi no owari ni*

ここはどこですか?
koko wa doko desuka
Where are we?

5 Say it (2 minutes)

Turn right at the traffic lights.

Turn left at the station.

It's about ten minutes.

信号を左に曲がって
ください。
shingoh o hidari ni magatte kudasai

Turn left at the traffic lights.

遠いですか?
toh-i desuka

Is it far?

いいえ、5分くらいです。
ihe, go fun kurai desu

No, it's about five minutes.

KANKOH
Sightseeing

Say the days of the week in Japanese. (pp.28-29)

How do you say "six o'clock"? (pp.30-31)

Ask "What time is it?" (pp.30-31)

Japanese stores open late and close around 10 or 11 p.m. The main closing days for tourist sights are Sunday or Monday. However, urban Japan is a 24/7 society, and you will generally find a few *konbini* (abbreviated from *convenience stores*) and cafés open whatever the time of day or night.

2 **Words to remember** (4 minutes)

Familiarize yourself with these words and test yourself using the flap.

ガイドブック *gaido bukku*	guidebook
入場無料 *nyu-jyo muryoh*	free entrance
開館時間 *kaikan jikan*	opening times (museums, libraries)
営業時間 *eigyoh jikan*	opening times (stores, restaurants)
休日 *kyu jitsu*	public holiday

ガイド付きツアー
gaido tsuki tsuah
guided tour

Cultural tip There are many unusual free attractions in Japan. These include beer, sake, and fishcake museums; wine cellars; food factories; galleries; electronics and cosmetics showrooms; and even television and film studios.

3 **In conversation** (3 minutes)

今日の午後は開いていますか?
kyoh no gogo wa aite imasuka

Do you open this afternoon?

はい、でも六時には閉まります。
hai, demo roku ji niwa shimari masu

Yes, but we close at six o'clock.

車いすは使えますか?
kurumaisu wa tsukae masuka

Is wheelchair access possible?

4 Useful phrases (3 minutes)

Learn these phrases and then test yourself using the cover flap.

What time do you open?	何時に開きますか? *nanji ni akimasuka*
What time does the store close?	店は何時に 閉まりますか? *mise wa nanji ni shimari masuka*
Is wheelchair access possible?	車いすは使えますか? *kurumaisu wa tsukae masuka*

5 Put into practice (4 minutes)

Cover the text on the right and complete the dialogue in Japanese.

すみません。博物館は閉館
しました。
*sumimasen. hakubutsu kan
wa heikan shimashita*

Sorry. The museum is closed.

Ask: Do you open
on Sundays?

日曜日はオープンして
いますか?
*nichiyo bi wa ohpun
shite imasuka*

はい、でも早く閉館します。
*hai, demo hayaku
heikan shimasu*

Yes, but we close early.

Ask: At what time?

何時にですか?
nanji ni desuka

はい。あちらに
エレベーターがあります。
*hai. achira ni erebehtah
ga arimasu*

Yes, there's an elevator
over there.

ありがとう。
チケットを四枚
お願いします。
*arigatoh. chiketto o
yonmai onegai shimasu*

Thank you. I'd like
four tickets.

どうぞ。ガイドブックは
無料です。
*dohzo. gaido bukku wa
muryoh desu*

Here you are. The
guidebook is free.

Say "Would you please help me?" (pp.24–25)

What's the Japanese for "ticket"? (pp.38–39)

Say "I'm going to Osaka." (pp.40–41)

KU-KOH DE
At the airport

International flights arrive at Tokyo's Narita airport, and an extensive network of internal flights operate out of the domestic Haneda airport. Although the airport environment is largely universal, it is sometimes useful to be able to understand key words and phrases in Japanese.

2 **Words to remember** (4 minutes)

Familiarize yourself with these words and test yourself using the flap.

チェックイン *chekku in*	check-in
出発 *shuppatsu*	departures
到着 *tohchaku*	arrivals
税関 *zeikan*	customs
入国審査 / 出国審査 *nyu-koku shinsa/ shukkoku shinsa*	passport control (entering/leaving Japan)
ターミナル *tahminaru*	terminal
搭乗口 *tohjyoh guchi*	gate
…便 *bin*	flight number …

香港行きの飛行機は
どこの搭乗口ですか?
*honkon iki no hikohki
wa doko no tohjyoh
guchi desuka*
Which gate is the flight
to Hong Kong?

3 **Useful phrases** (3 minutes)

Learn these phrases and then test yourself using the cover flap.

ロンドンからの飛行機 は予定通りですか? *Rondon kara no hikohki wa yotei dohri desuka*	Is the flight from London on time?

荷物が見つかり ません。 *nimotsu ga mitsukari masen*	I can't find my luggage.

京都への飛行機は 遅れています。 *Kyoto eno hikohki wa okurete imasu*	The flight to Kyoto is delayed.

4 Put into practice (3 minutes)

Join in this conversation. Read the Japanese on the left and follow the instructions to make your reply. Then test yourself by concealing the answers with the cover flap.

次の方どうぞ。
tsugi no kata dohzo

Next, please.

京都への飛行機は予定通りですか?
Kyoto eno hikohki wa yotei dohri desuka

Ask: Is the flight to Kyoto on time?

はい。予定通りです。
hai. yotei dohri desu

Yes, it's on time.

どの搭乗口ですか?
dono tohjyoh guchi desuka

Ask: Which gate is it?

5 Match and repeat (4 minutes)

Match the numbered items to the Japanese words in the panel.

❶ 搭乗券
tohjyoh ken

❷ チケット
chiketto

❸ パスポート
pasupohto

❹ スーツケース
su-tsu kehsu

❺ カート
kahto

boarding ❶ pass

ticket ❷

passport ❸

suitcase   ❺ cart

空港 *ku-koh* airport

Read it Here's another example of two *kanji* characters combining to make a separate meaning: 空 (*ku*, sky) + 港 (*koh*, port).

FUKUSHU TO KURIKAESHI
Review and repeat

1 Places

❶ 博物館
hakubutsu kan

❷ 横断歩道
ohdan hodoh

❸ 橋
hashi

❹ 寺
tera

❺ 駐車場
chusha jyo

❻ 映画館
eiga kan

❼ 広場
hiroba

1 Places (4 minutes)

Name the numbered places in Japanese.

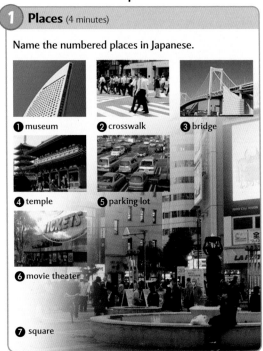

❶ museum   ❷ crosswalk   ❸ bridge

❹ temple   ❺ parking lot

❻ movie theater

❼ square

2 Car parts

❶ フロントガラス
furonto garasu

❷ ヘッドライト
heddo raito

❸ バンパー
banpah

❹ ドア
doa

❺ タイヤ
taiya

2 Car parts (3 minutes)

Name these car parts in Japanese.

windshield ❶

bumper ❸

tire ❺

❹ door

3 Translation (4 minutes)

What do these Japanese phrases mean?

❶ *hidari ni magatte kudasai*

❷ *kono machi ni hakubutsu kan wa arimasuka*

❸ *mantan de onegai shimasu*

❹ *koko wa doko desuka*

❺ *hashi no chikaku ni suimingu puhru ga arimasu*

❻ *nanji ni akimasuka*

❼ *chiketto o yonmai onegai shimasu*

3 Translation

❶ (Please) turn left.

❷ Is there a museum in town?

❸ Fill it up, please.

❹ Where are we?

❺ There's a swimming pool near the bridge.

❻ What time do you open?

❼ I'd like four tickets.

❷ headlight

4 Directions (4 minutes)

Ask how to get to these places:

❶ temple
❷ station
❸ internet café
❹ movie theater

4 Directions

❶ 寺にはどうやって
行けばいいですか?
*tera niwa dohyatte
ikeba iidesuka*

❷ 駅にはどうやって
行けばいいですか?
*eki niwa dohyatte
ikeba iidesuka*

❸ ネットカフェにはどう
やって行けば
いいですか?
*netto kafeh niwa
dohyatte ikeba
iidesuka*

❹ 映画館にはどう
やって行けばいいで
すか?
*eiga kan niwa
dohyatte ikeba
iidesuka*

HEYA NO YOYAKU
Booking a room

Ask "How much is that?"
(pp.18-19)

What are "breakfast,"
"lunch," and "dinner"?
(pp.20-21)

What are "three," "four,"
"five," and "six"? (pp.10-11)

Japan has a large number of international hotels, as
well as the traditional Japanese inns (see pp.62-63).
Rabuhoteru (*love hotels*) rentable by the hour are best
avoided. The famous tubular *kapuseruhoteru* (*capsule
hotels*) are also available in major cities but aren't
suitable for the claustrophobic.

2 Useful phrases (3 minutes)

Practice these phrases and then test yourself by
concealing the Japanese on the left with the cover flap.

朝食込みですか?
chohshoku komi desuka

Is breakfast included?

部屋からインターネットに
アクセスできますか?
*heya kara intahnetto ni
akusesu dekimasuka*

Does the room have
internet access?

ルームサービス
はありますか?
*ru-mu sahbisu
wa arimasuka*

Is there room service?

チェックアウトは
何時ですか?
*chekkuauto wa
nanji desuka*

What time is checkout?

3 In conversation (5 minutes)

空いている部屋は
ありますか?
*aiteiru heya wa
arimasuka*

Do you have
any rooms?

はい。ダブルルーム
がございます。
*hai. daburu ru-mu ga
gozaimasu*

Yes, we have a
double room.

ルームサービス
はありますか?
*ru-mu sahbisu
wa arimasuka*

Is there room service?

4 Words to remember (4 minutes)

Familiarize yourself with these words and test yourself by concealing the Japanese on the right with the cover flap.

部屋から海が見えますか?
heya kara umi ga mie masuka
Does the room have an ocean view?

5 Say it (2 minutes)

Do you have any single rooms?

For two nights.

Is dinner included?

room	部屋	*heya*
single room	シングルルーム	*shinguru ru-mu*
double room	ダブルルーム	*daburu ru-mu*
twin room	ツインルーム	*tsuin ru-mu*
bathroom	バス	*basu*
shower	シャワー	*shawah*
breakfast	朝食	*chohshoku*
key	キー	*kih*
balcony	バルコニー	*barukonih*
two nights	二泊	*ni haku*
three nights	三泊	*san paku*

 Cultural tip Japanese hotel rooms tend to include a pair of house slippers as a matter of course. You are assumed to want to remove your shoes in the room, as you would at home. Hotel staff address customers using ultra-polite, uncommon Japanese expressions.

はい。何泊のご予定
ですか?
hai. nan paku no goyoteh desuka

Yes. How many nights?

三泊です。
san paku desu

For three nights.

かしこまりました。
これがキーです。
kashikomari mashita. kore ga kih desu

Very good. Here's your key.

HOTERU DE
In the hotel

1 **Warm up** (1 minute)

How do you say "Is/Are there ...?," "There is/are ...," and "There isn't/aren't ..."? (pp.48–49)

What's the Japanese for "room"? (pp.58–59)

As well as slippers, you will nearly always find a traditional Japanese *robe/pajamas* (**yukata**) in your room—usually laid out on the bed. This is the case even in the international chains. Nonsmoking rooms are sometimes offered, but exclusively nonsmoking floors are not always available.

2 **Match and repeat** (6 minutes)

Match the numbered items in this hotel bedroom with the Japanese text in the panel and test yourself using the cover flap.

1 ベッドサイド
テーブル
beddo saido tehburu

2 ランプ
ranpu

3 ミニバー
minibah

4 カーテン
kahten

5 ソファ
sofa

6 枕
makura

7 ベッド
beddo

8 ベッドスプレッド
beddo supureddo

9 毛布
mohfu

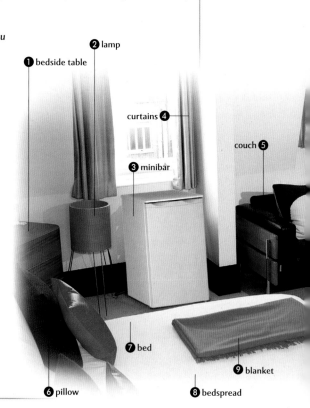

2 lamp
1 bedside table
curtains **4**
couch **5**
3 minibar
7 bed
9 blanket
6 pillow
8 bedspread

Cultural tip Japanese bathrooms can be a culture shock to visitors. The bathtubs are smaller, as they are generally only used for soaping yourself before rinsing under the shower. The toilets often feature high-tech gadgets, such as heated seats. Some even act as automatic bidets, with an built-in washer and dryer.

3 Useful phrases (5 minutes)

Learn these phrases and then test yourself using the cover flap.

The room is too hot. 部屋が暑すぎます。
heya ga atsu sugi masu

The room is too cold. 部屋が寒すぎます。
heya ga samu sugi masu

There aren't any towels. タオルが
ありません。
taoru ga arimasen

I'd like some soap. 石けんを下さい。
sekken o kudasai

The shower seems to be broken. シャワーが壊れて
いるようです。
shawah ga kowarete iruyoh desu

4 Put into practice (3 minutes)

Cover the text on the right and then complete the dialogue in Japanese.

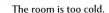

はい、フロントで
ございます。
hai, furonto de gozaimasu

Yes, front desk.

枕はありますか?
makura wa arimasuka

Say: Are there any pillows?

部屋の担当者が
持って参ります。
heya no tantoh-sha ga motte mairimasu

The staff will bring you some.

それからテレビが壊れて
いるようです。
sorekara terebi ga kowarete iruyoh desu

Say: And the television seems to be broken.

RYOKAN TO ONSEN
Inns and spas

What is Japanese for "shower" (pp.60-61) and "swimming pool"? (pp.48-49)

Say "I'd like some towels." (pp.60-61)

Traditional Japanese inns, **ryokan**, and spas with hot springs, **onsen**, are often based in beautiful surroundings and offer a haven of peace. Prices are usually inclusive of accommodations and all meals. Additional health treatments such as massage are often also available.

2 Match and repeat (4 minutes)

Learn these phrases and then test yourself by concealing the Japanese with the cover flap.

❶ ふすま
fusuma

❷ 浴衣
yukata

❸ 鏡台
kyodai

❹ 障子
shoji

❺ 畳
tatami

❻ 布団
futon

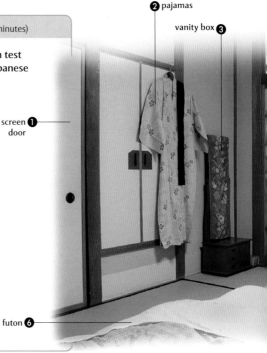

❷ pajamas

vanity box ❸

screen ❶
door

futon ❻

3 In conversation (5 minutes)

二泊したいのですが。
ni haku shitai no desuga

I'd like to stay for two nights.

かしこまりました。
kashikomari mashita

Certainly.

この旅館に温泉は
ありますか?
kono ryokan ni onsen wa arimasuka

Is there a hot spring (tub) in the inn?

4 Say it (2 minutes)

I'd like to stay for five nights.

Is there a swimming pool in the inn?

Can I rent *yukata* pajamas?

5 Useful phrases (3 minutes)

Learn these phrases. Read the English under the pictures and say the phrase in Japanese as shown on the right. Then cover up the answers on the right and test yourself.

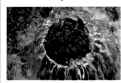

どんなタイプの温泉
ですか？
*donna taipu no
onsen desuka*

What type of hot springs do you have?

サウナはありますか？
sauna wa arimasuka

Is there a sauna?

マッサージを予約
できますか？
*massahji o yoyaku
dekimasuka*

Can I book a massage?

タオルを借りることが
できますか？
*taoru o karirukoto
ga dekimasuka*

Can I rent a towel?

❹ screen window

❺ tatami mat

はい。屋上に
ございます。
*hai. okujoh ni
gozaimasu*

Yes, it's located on the roof.

タオルを借りることが
できますか？
*taoru o karirukoto ga
dekimasuka*

Can I rent a towel?

入り口で貸し出して
おります。
*iriguchi de kashidashite
orimasu*

You can rent one at the spa entrance.

1 Warm up (1 minute)

How do you say
"My son has a car"?
(pp.14-15)

What is the Japanese
for "room," "bed," and
"pillow"? (pp.60-61)

KEIYOH-SHI
Adjectives

Basic adjectives (descriptive words) are quite simple to use in Japanese: car(s) is **kuruma**; small car(s) is **chihsai kuruma**. In a sentence, the word order is: item(s) + **wa/ga** (as for) + adjective + **desu**—for example, **kuruma wa chihsai desu** (The car is small); **yama wa takai desu** (The mountains are high).

2 Words to remember (7 minutes)

There are no plurals in Japanese. So *the mountain is high* and *the mountains are high* would both be *yama wa takai desu*.

大きい *ohkih*	big, large
小さい *chihsai*	small
高い *takai*	high, tall
低い *hikui*	short
暑い *atsui*	hot
冷たい *tsumetai*	cold
静か *shizuka*	quiet
うるさい *urusai*	noisy
硬い *katai*	hard
柔らかい *yawarakai*	soft
美しい *utsukushih*	beautiful

山は高いです。
yama wa takai desu
The mountains
are high.

森が綺麗です。
mori ga kireh desu
The forest is
beautiful.

寺は古いです。
tera wa furui desu
The temple is old.

あの橋はとても狭いです。
ano hashi wa totemo semai desu
That bridge is very narrow.

Read it All of the adjectives above except *noisy* are written in a mixture of *kanji* and *hiragana* characters. The first *kanji* character carries the core meaning—for example, 大 (big), 美 (beautiful). The attached *hiragana* characters are grammatical endings. Look up the *hiragana* characters in the table on pp.158-159 to identify the syllables they represent.

3 Useful phrases (4 minutes)

You can emphasize a description by using *totemo* (very) before the adjective: *totemo urusai* (very noisy).

The coffee is cold.	コーヒーが冷たいです。 *koh-hi ga tsumetai desu*
My room is very noisy.	私の部屋はとてもうるさいです。 *watashi no heya wa totemo urusai desu*
This car is very small.	この車はとても小さいです。 *kono kuruma wa totemo chihsai desu*
This bed is hard.	このベッドは硬いです。 *kono beddo wa katai desu*

4 Put into practice (3 minutes)

Join in this conversation. Cover up the text on the right and complete the dialogue in Japanese. Check and repeat if necessary.

こちらが部屋です。
kochira ga heya desu
Here's the room.

Say: The view is very beautiful.

景色がとても美しいです。
keshiki ga totemo utsukushih desu

バスルームはあちらです。
basu ru-mu wa achira desu
The bathroom is over there.

Say: It's very small.

とても小さいです。
totemo chihsai desu

あいにく他には部屋はございません。
ainiku hoka niwa heya wa gozaimasen
Unfortunately, there aren't any other rooms.

Say: We'll take it.

これにします。
kore ni shimasu

Kotae
Answers (Cover with flap)

FUKUSHU TO KURIKAESHI
Review and repeat

1 Adjectives

❶ 大きい
ohkih

❷ 柔らかい
yawarakai

❸ 古い
furui

❹ 静か
shizuka

❺ 冷たい
tsumetai

1 Adjectives (3 minutes)

Put the word in parentheses into Japanese.

❶ *ie wa _____ desu.* (big)

❷ *beddo wa _____ desu.* (soft)

❸ *tera wa totemo _____ desu.* (old)

❹ *watashi no heya wa _____ desu.* (quiet)

❺ *mizu ga totemo _____ desu.* (cold)

2 Inns

❶ ふすま
fusuma

❷ 浴衣
yukata

❸ 鏡台
kyodai

❹ 布団
futon

❺ 障子
shoji

❻ 畳
tatami

2 Inns (3 minutes)

Name these items you might find in a traditional Japanese inn.

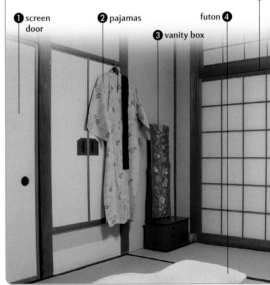

❺ screen window

❶ screen door

❷ pajamas

❸ vanity box

❹ futon

3 At the hotel (4 minutes)

You are booking a room in a hotel. Follow the conversation, replying in Japanese using the English prompts.

hai, dohzo

❶ Do you have any rooms?

hai. nanpaku no goyoteh desuka

❷ Five nights.

kashikomari mashita

❸ Is breakfast included?

ihe. go-hyaku yen desu

❹ We'll take it.

3 At the hotel

❶ 空いている部屋は
ありますか?
*aiteiru heya wa
arimasuka*

❷ 五泊です。
go haku desu

❸ 朝食込みですか?
*chohshoku komi
desuka*

❹ これにします。
kore ni shimasu

4 Negatives (5 minutes)

Make these sentences negative using *wa arimasen*.

❶ *taoru wa arimasu*

❷ *ru-mu sahbisu wa arimasu*

❸ *kono ryokan ni onsen
wa arimasu*

❹ *kono machi ni hakubutsu
kan wa arimasu*

❺ *meishi wa arimasu*

tatami mat ❻

4 Negatives

❶ タオルは
ありません。
taoru wa arimasen

❷ ルームサービス
はありません。
*ru-mu sahbisu wa
arimasen*

❸ この旅館に温泉は
ありません。
*kono ryokan ni onsen
wa arimasen*

❹ この街に博物館は
ありません。
*kono machi ni
hakubutsu kan wa
arimasen*

❺ 名刺はありません。
meishi wa arimasen

1 Warm up (1 minute)

Ask "Can I use a credit card?" (p.39)

Say "Turn left at the traffic lights" and "The station is near the café." (pp.50-51)

DEPAHTO
Department store

In recent years, many Japanese have started buying food and other provisions in **depahto**. The basement floor of department stores usually houses a food "market" with separate stalls. However, many towns also have shopping malls, often adjacent to local train stations.

2 Match and repeat (5 minutes)

Notice the Japanese word *ya*, meaning *shop*: *pan ya*, bread shop (bakery); *niku ya*, meat shop (butcher), etc. Match the shops numbered 1-9 on the right to the Japanese in the panel.

❶ パン屋
pan ya

❷ ケーキ屋
kehki ya

❸ 酒屋
saka ya

❹ デリカテッセン
derikatessen

❺ 八百屋
yao ya

❻ 本屋
hon ya

❼ 魚屋
sakana ya

❽ 肉屋
niku ya

❾ 豆腐屋
tofu ya

❶ bakery

❷ cake shop

❹ delicatessen

❺ produce market

❼ seafood shop

❽ butcher

Cultural tip Department stores will often have a folk art section (*kyohdo zaiku*). Here, you can buy traditional souvenirs such as painted wooden dolls, lanterns, fans, kimonos, parasols, screens, and origami kits. You can also find the famous Japanese **nurimono** (lacquer ware) in the form of decorated bowls, boxes, and pots with natural designs (flowers, birds, etc.). All of these make very good gifts.

花屋はどこですか?
hana ya wa doko desuka
Where's the florist?

❸ liquor store

❻ bookstore

❾ tofu shop

5 Say it (2 minutes)

Where's the bakery?

Do you have towels?

I'd like to place an order for curtains.

3 Words to remember (4 minutes)

Familiarize yourself with these words and then test yourself.

dairy	乳製品 *nyu seihin*
antique store	骨董品店 *kotto hin ten*
beauty salon	美容院 *biyoh in*
barbershop	理容院 *riyoh in*
jewelry store	宝石商 *hohseki shoh*
post office	郵便局 *yu-bin kyoku*
florist	花屋 *hana ya*
shoe store	靴屋 *kutsu ya*
travel agency	旅行代理店 *ryokoh dairi ten*

4 Useful phrases (3 minutes)

Familiarize yourself with these phrases.

Where's the beauty salon?	美容院はどこですか? *biyoh in wa doko desuka*
Where can I pay?	どこで払えますか? *doko de harae masuka*
I'm just looking. Thanks.	見ているだけです。 どうも。 *mite iru dake desu.* *dohmo*
Do you sell SIM cards?	SIMカードを売っていますか? *simu cahdo o utte imasuka*
Can I exchange this?	交換できますか? *kohkan dekimasuka*
Can you give me the receipt?	レシートをもらえますか? *reshihto o morae masuka*
I'd like to place an order for ...	...を注文したいです。 *...o chu-mon shitai desu*

DENKIYA
Electronics store

Tokyo is home to probably the world's largest concentration of electronics stores in the famous Akihabara "electric town." Here you can find a huge range of computers, cameras, gadgets, and parts, both new and second-hand. Guarantees vary, and you need to check the equipment will work at home.

1 Warm up (1 minute)

What are "forty," "seventy," "a hundred," "a thousand," and "ten thousand" in Japanese? (pp.30-31)

Say "big" and "small" in Japanese. (pp.64-65)

2 Match and repeat (4 minutes)

Match the numbered items to the Japanese words in the panel below and test yourself using the cover flap.

❶ マウス
mausu

❷ アダプタ
adaputa

❸ 変圧器
hen-atsuki

❹ パソコン
pasokon

❺ 画面
gamen

❻ ハードドライブ
hahdo doraibu

❼ USB フラッシュドライブ
USB furasshu doraibu

Read it When you see price labels, you will usually see the symbol for *yen* (¥), or sometimes the character 円, with the price in Western figures. The full-stop and dash after the amount mean *and no more*.

¥9,950.–   299円

hard drive ❻   transformer ❸

❼ USB flash drive   ❶ mouse

3 In conversation (5 minutes)

あのパソコンは
いくらですか?
ano pasokon wa ikura desuka

How much is that laptop computer?

税込み10万円です。
zeikomi jyu-man yen desu

It's 100,000 yen, including tax.

ハードディスクの
容量はいくらですか?
hahdo disuku no yoryo wa ikura desuka

How big is the hard drive?

Cultural tip The Japanese currency system is the *yen* (¥). As each yen is worth less than 1 cent, you'll generally be spending thousands or even tens of thousands of them. Bill denominations go up to ¥10,000, so be careful not to confuse the number of zeros.

4 laptop

5 screen

2 adapter

4 Useful phrases (5 minutes)

Learn these phrases. Then conceal the answers on the right using the cover flap. Read the English under the pictures and say the phrase in Japanese as shown on the right.

あのカメラは
高すぎます。
*ano kamera wa
takasugi masu*

That camera is
too expensive.

あれはいくら
ですか?
a-re wa ikura desuka

How much is that one?

イギリスで使え
ますか?
igirisu de tsukae masuka

Will it work in England?

500ギガで、メモリーは8
ギガです。
*gohyaku giga de momori wa
hachi giga desu*

500 gigabytes, and 8
gigabytes of memory.

イギリスで使え
ますか?
igirisu de tsukae masuka

Will it work in England?

はい。ただし変圧器が必要
です。
*hai. tadashi hen-atsuki ga
hitsuyo desu*

Yes, but you need
a transformer.

SU-PAH DE
At the supermarket

What are these items, which you could buy in a supermarket? (pp.22-23)

yasai
kudamono
shifudo
kome
wain
mizu

Japanese supermarkets are often more like hypermarkets, selling household items and clothes, as well as food and essentials. Most Japanese still pay for their groceries in cash. Paying by card at a supermarket is still not common, but cards are frequently used in other stores, such as clothing stores.

2 **Match and repeat** (5 minutes)

Look at the numbered items and match them to the Japanese words in the panel below.

❶ 家庭用品
kateh yo-hin

❷ 果物
kudamono

❸ 飲み物
nomimono

❹ 加工食品
kakoh shokuhin

❺ 野菜
yasai

❻ 冷凍食品
reitoh shokuhin

❼ 菓子類
kashi rui

❽ 化粧品
keshoh hin

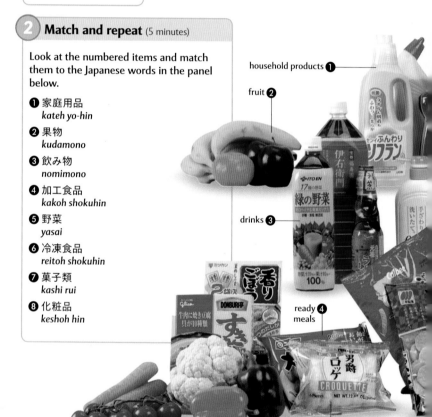

household products ❶

fruit ❷

drinks ❸

ready ❹
meals

vegetables ❺

frozen foods ❻

Cultural tip Supermarkets usually prepackage fresh produce such as meat, fish, fruits, vegetables, and cheese. You just pick up the prepriced package you want and take it to the checkout.

3 Useful phrases (3 minutes)

Learn these phrases and then test yourself using the cover flap.

May I have a bag, please?	ビニール袋をもらえますか？ *binihru bukuro o moraemasuka*
Where's the liquor aisle?	飲み物類はどこですか？ *nomimono rui wa doko desuka*
Where's the checkout?	レジはどこですか？ *reji wa doko desuka*
Where are the shopping carts?	ショッピングカートはどこですか？ *shoppingu kahto wa doko desuka*

8 beauty products

7 snacks

4 Words to remember (4 minutes)

Learn these words and then test yourself using the cover flap.

bread	パン *pan*
milk	牛乳 *gyu-nyu*
butter	バター *batah*
dairy products	乳製品 *nyu seihin*
ham	ハム *hamu*
salt	塩 *shio*
pepper	胡椒 *koshoh*
toilet paper	トイレットペーパー *toiretto pehpah*
diapers	オムツ *omutsu*
dishwashing liquid	食器用洗剤 *shokki yoh senzai*

5 Say it (2 minutes)

Where's the toilet paper?

May I have some butter, please?

Is there any ham?

FUKU TO KUTSU
Clothes and shoes

Say "A ..., please."
(pp.24-25)

Ask "Is there a ...?"
(pp.48-49)

Say "thirteen," "twenty-four," and "thirty" in Japanese. (pp.30-31)

Say "big" and "small" in Japanese. (pp.64-65)

Loan words are used for most Western-style clothes: **pantsu** (*pants*), **jyaketto** (*jacket*), etc. Only items that existed traditionally have Japanese names: **kutsu** (*shoes*), **sode** (*sleeves*). Other traditional articles, such as the **kimono**, **obi** (*sash*), and **geta** (*clogs*) are now largely reserved for special occasions.

Match the numbered items of clothing to the Japanese words in the panel below. Test yourself using the cover flap.

❶ シャツ
shatsu

❷ ネクタイ
nekutai

❸ 袖
sode

❹ ジャケット
jyaketto

❺ ポケット
poketto

❻ パンツ
pantsu

❼ スカート
sukahto

❽ ストッキング
sutokkingu

❾ 靴
kutsu

shirt ❶

tie ❷

sleeve ❸

jacket ❹

pocket ❺

pants ❻

Cultural tip Japan has its own system of sizes. Generally, for women's clothes, add two to get Japanese sizes. For example, US size 10 is Japanese 12 and US 12 is Japanese 14. A Japanese shoe size 23 is roughly equivalent to a size 4, 24 is a size 5, etc. Even allowing for conversion of sizes, Japanese clothes tend to be cut very small.

3 Useful phrases (5 minutes)

Learn these phrases and then test yourself using the cover flap.

Do you have a larger size?	もっと大きいサイズが ありますか? *motto ohkih saizu ga arimasuka*
It's not what I want.	わたしが欲しいものでは ありません。 *watashi ga hoshih mono dewa arimasen*
I'll take the pink one.	ピンクのを買い ます。 *pinku no o kaimasu*

4 Words to remember (5 minutes)

Colors are adjectives (see p.64). Below you will see the pure form of the colors, but you may find that endings have been added to the word depending on the sentence.

red	赤	*aka*
white	白	*shiro*
blue	青	*ao*
yellow	黄色	*ki iro*
green	緑	*midori*
black	黒	*kuro*

❼ skirt

❽ pantyhose

❾ shoes

Read it All the items of clothing in section 2, except *shoes* and *sleeve*, are written in **katakana**, the script used for foreign loan words. Use the **katakana** table on pp.158-159 to work out the syllables in each word.

FUKUSHU TO KURIKAESHI
Review and repeat

1 Electronic

❶ マウス
mausu

❷ アダプタ
adaputa

❸ 変圧器
hen-atsuki

❹ パソコン
pasokon

❺ 画面
gamen

❻ ハードドライブ
hahdo doraibu

❼ USB フラッシュドライブ
USB furasshu doraibu

1 Electronic (3 minutes)

Name the numbered items in Japanese.

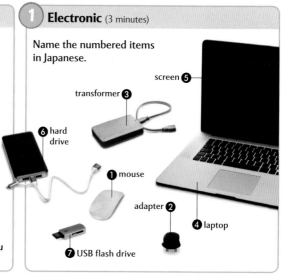

screen ❺

transformer ❸

❻ hard drive

❶ mouse

adapter ❷

❹ laptop

❼ USB flash drive

2 Description

❶ That camera is too expensive.

❷ My room is very noisy.

❸ Do you have a larger size?

2 Description (2 minutes)

What do these phrases mean?

❶ *ano kamera wa takasugi masu*

❷ *watashi no heya wa totemo urusai desu*

❸ *motto ohkih saizu ga arimasuka*

3 Shops

❶ パン屋
pan ya

❷ デリカテッセン
derikatessen

❸ 八百屋
yao ya

❹ 魚屋
sakana ya

❺ ケーキ屋
kehki ya

❻ 肉屋
niku ya

3 Shops (3 minutes)

Name the numbered shops in Japanese. Then check your answers.

❶ bakery

❷ delicatessen

❸ produce market

❹ seafood shop

❺ cake shop

❻ butcher

4 Supermarket (3 minutes)

What is the Japanese for the numbered product categories?

❶ household products

❷ beauty products

❸ drinks

❹ snacks

❺ frozen foods

4 Supermarket

❶ 家庭用品
kateh yo-hin

❷ 化粧品
keshoh hin

❸ 飲み物
nomimono

❹ 菓子類
kashi rui

❺ 冷凍食品
reitoh shokuhin

5 Museum (4 minutes)

Join in this conversation, replying in Japanese following the English prompts.

> *hai, dohzo*

❶ I'd like four tickets.

> *happyaku yen ni narimasu*

❷ What time do you close?

> *roku ji ni shimari masu*

❸ Is there a guidebook?

> *dohzo. gaido bukku wa muryoh desu*

❹ Where's the elevator?

> *achira ni erebehtah ga arimasu*

❺ Thank you very much.

5 Museum

❶ チケットを四枚お願いします。
chiketto o yonmai onegai shimasu

❷ 何時に閉まりますか？
nanji ni shimarimasuka

❸ ガイドブックはありますか？
gaido bukku wa arimasuka

❹ エレベーターはどこですか？
erebehtah wa doko desuka

❺ どうもありがとうございます。
dohmo arigatoh gozaimasu

SHIGOTO
Jobs

1 Warm up (1 minute)

Say "Akiko is a student" and "I'm British." (pp.14-15)

Say "The internet café is in the center of town." (pp.48-49)

Japanese has some generic, non-job-specific words used to refer mainly to office workers–the self-explanatory **sararihman** (salary man) and the **OL** (pronounced "oh-el" and meaning office lady) being two of the most common. **Sengyo-shufu** (literally specialist) is used to mean housewife.

2 Words to remember: jobs (7 minutes)

Familiarize yourself with these Japanese words and test yourself using the flap.

医者 *isha*	doctor
歯医者 *ha-isha*	dentist
看護師 *kangoshi*	nurse
先生 *sensei*	teacher
会計士 *kaikehshi*	accountant
弁護士 *bengoshi*	lawyer
デザイナー *dezainah*	designer
秘書 *hisho*	secretary
店主 *tenshu*	retailer
電気技師 *denki gishi*	electrician
配管工 *haikankoh*	plumber
コック *kokku*	cook
自営業 *ji-eigyoh*	self-employed
学生 *gakusei*	student

会社員です。
kaisha in desu
I'm a businessman.

会計士です。
kaikehshi desu
I'm an accountant.

3 Put into practice (4 minutes)

Join in this conversation. Use the cover flap to conceal the text on the right and complete the dialogue in Japanese.

ご職業は?
goshokugyoh wa

会計士です。
kaikehshi desu

What's your profession?

Say: I'm an accountant.

どの会社にお勤めですか?
doko no kaisha ni otsutomete desuka

自営業です。
ji-eigyoh desu

What company do you work for?

Say: I'm self-employed.

ああ、そうなんですか!
ah, sohnandesuka

ご職業は?
goshokugyoh wa

Oh, really!

Ask: What's your profession?

Cultural tip There are different titles for manager depending on the level. The order of seniority is 社長 *shacho* (MD), 専務 *senmu* (division), 部長 *bucho* (department), 課長 *kacho* (section), 係長 *kakaricho* (team). Look out for the titles on business cards.

4 Words to remember: workplace (3 minutes)

本社は大阪にあります
honsha wa Osaka ni arimasu
The headquarters is in Osaka.

Familiarize yourself with these words and test yourself.

headquarters	本社 *honsha*
branch	支店 *shiten*
... department	...部 *...bu*
office worker	会社員 *kaisha in*
manager	マネージャー *manehjyah*

OFISU
The office

1 Warm up (1 minute)

Practice different ways of introducing yourself in different situations (pp.8-9). Mention your name, occupation, and any other information you'd like to volunteer (pp.12-13, pp.14-15).

Traditionally, most adult Japanese would have an *inkan*—an official seal or stamp unique to the individual and used to sign papers and forms. You may still see these stamps on official government papers and high-level contracts, although they are no longer the necessity they once were.

2 Words to remember (5 minutes)

Familiarize yourself with these words. Read them aloud several times and try to memorize them. Conceal the Japanese with the cover flap and test yourself.

コンピュータ *konpyu-tah*	computer
マウス *mausu*	mouse
メール *mehru*	email
インターネット *intahnetto*	internet
パスワード *pasuwahdo*	password
ボイスメール *boisu mehru*	voicemail
ワイファイパスワード *wai fai pasuwahdo*	Wi-Fi password
コピー *kopih*	photocopy
コピー機 *kopihki*	photocopier ("copy machine")
本 *hon*	book
手帳 *techoh*	daily planner
名刺 *meishi*	business card
ミーティング *mihtingu*	meeting
コンフェレンス *konferensu*	conference
会議事項 *kaigi jikoh*	agenda

lamp ①
screen ④
laptop ⑥
keyboard ⑤
② stapler
telephone ③
drawer ⑫
pen ⑩   ⑪ notepad
desk ⑦

3 Useful phrases (2 minutes)

Learn these phrases and then test yourself using the cover flap.

I need to make some photocopies.	コピーをとる必要が あります。 *kopih o toru hitsuyoh ga arimasu*
I'd like to arrange an appointment.	アポを取りたいの ですが。 *apo o toritai no desuga*
I want to send an email.	メールを送りたい です。 *mehru o okuritai desu*

4 Match and repeat (5 minutes)

Match the numbered items to the Japanese words on the right.

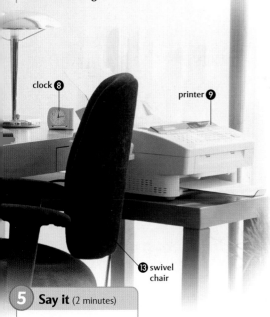

clock **8**

printer **9**

13 swivel chair

❶ ランプ
ranpu

❷ ホチキス
hochikisu

❸ 電話
denwa

❹ 画面
gamen

❺ キーボード
kihbohdo

❻ パソコン
pasokon

❼ 机
tsukue

❽ 時計
tokei

❾ プリンター
purintah

❿ ペン
pen

⓫ ノート
nohto

⓬ 引き出し
hikidashi

⓭ 回転椅子
kaiten isu

5 Say it (2 minutes)

I'd like to arrange a meeting.

Do you have a business card?

Is there an agenda?

GAKKAI DE
At the conference

1 Warm up (1 minute)

Say "Oh, really?" (pp.78-79), "meeting" (pp.80-81), and "appointment." (pp.32-33)

Ask "What's your profession?" and answer "I'm a lawyer." (pp.78-79)

University courses usually last four years, and entrance to the top colleges is very competitive. High schools often start to prepare for the entrance exam many years in advance, as future prospects can depend on which university a student attends. Once there, the pressure is less intense.

2 Useful phrases (3 minutes)

Learn these phrases and then test yourself using the cover flap.

ご専門は？ *gosenmon wa*	What's your field?
研究をしています。 *kenkyu o shiteimasu*	I'm doing research.
法律を勉強しました。 *hohritsu o benkyoh shimashita*	I have a degree in law.
建築学の講師です。 *kenchiku gaku no kohshi desu*	I'm a lecturer in architecture.

3 In conversation (5 minutes)

こんにちは。岡田です。
konnichiwa. Okada desu

Hello, I'm Okada.

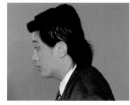

どこで教えていらっしゃいますか？
doko de oshiete irasshai masuka

Where do you teach?

東京大学です。
Tokyo daigaku desu

I teach at Tokyo University.

4 Words to remember (4 minutes)

Familiarize yourself with these words and then test yourself.

展示会には私達の
スタンドがあります。
*tenji kai niwa watashitachi
no sutando ga arimasu*
There's our exhibition stand.

conference (academic)	学会	*gakkai*
lecture	講義	*kohgi*
seminar	ゼミ	*zemi*
lecture hall	講堂	*kohdoh*
exhibition	展示会	*tenji kai*
university lecturer	大学講師	*daigaku kohshi*
professor	教授	*kyohjyu*
medicine	医学	*igaku*
science	科学	*kagaku*
literature	文学	*bungaku*
engineering	工学	*kohgaku*
law	法律	*hohritsu*
architecture	建築学	*kenchiku gaku*
information technology	IT	*"ai-tih"*

5 Say it (2 minutes)

I teach at Stanford University.

I have a degree in medicine.

I'm a lecturer in engineering.

ご専門は?
gosenmon wa

What's your field?

物理です。研究もしています。
butsuri desu. kenkyu mo shiteimasu

Physics. I'm also doing research.

ああ、そうですか?
ah, sohdesuka

Oh, really?

BIJINESU
In business

1 **Warm up** (1 minute)

Say "I want to send an email." (pp.80–81)

Say "I'd like to arrange an appointment." (pp.80–81)

You will make a good impression if you make the effort to begin a meeting with a few words in Japanese, even if your vocabulary is limited. After that, all parties will probably be happy to continue in English. Remember to take business cards to exchange at meetings.

2 **Words to remember** (6 minutes)

Familiarize yourself with these words and then test yourself by concealing the Japanese with the cover flap.

注文 *chu-mon*	order
配達 *haitatsu*	delivery
支払い *shiharai*	payment
予算 *yosan*	budget
値段 *nedan*	price
証書 *shohsho*	documents
請求書 *sehkyu-sho*	invoice
見積もり *mitsumori*	estimate
利益 *ri-eki*	profits
売り上げ *uri age*	sales
合計額 *gohkeh gaku*	figures

顧客
kokyaku
client

—— 報告書
hohkoku sho
report

Cultural tip In general, business dealings are formal. However, the Japanese are famous for their hospitality. Visitors are often escorted from the moment they wake up to the moment they go to bed. It's a good idea to take presents from home to show your appreciation.

契約書を見せてください。
kehyaku sho o misete kudasai
Please show me the contract.

重役
jyu-yaku
executive

3 Useful phrases (6 minutes)

Practice these phrases. Notice that the Japanese is necessarily very polite. It's better to err on the side of caution in a business context.

契約書を送ってください
ますか?
*kehyaku sho o okutte
kudasai masuka*

Can you send me the contract, please?

値段は決まりましたか?
nedan wa kimarimashitaka

Have we agreed on a price?

配達はいつになりますか?
*haitatsu wa itsu ni
nari masuka*

When can you make the delivery?

予算はおいくら
ですか?
yosan wa oikura desuka

What's the budget?

Read it Some traditional Japanese words used in a business context have alternative English loan words. These imported words will be written in *katakana* characters. For example, you may see the following alternatives for the traditional words in this lesson. See if you can work out the individual syllables of the words using the *katakana* table on pp.158-159.

オーダー *ohdah* order

ドキュメント *dokyumento* document

レポート *repohto* report

4 Say it (2 minutes)

Can you send me the invoice, please?

What's the price?

Please show me the order.

Kotae
Answers (Cover with flap)

FUKUSHU TO KURIKAESHI
Review and repeat

1 At the office

❶ ランプ
ranpu

❷ パソコン
pasokon

❸ ノート
nohto

❹ ホチキス
hochikisu

❺ 机
tsukue

❻ ペン
pen

❼ 時計
tokei

1 At the office (4 minutes)

Name these items in Japanese.

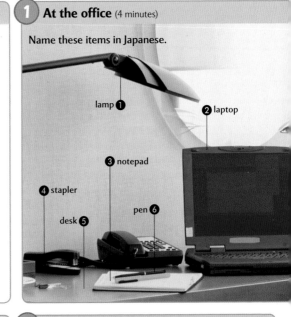

lamp ❶

❷ laptop

❸ notepad

❹ stapler

❺ desk

pen ❻

2 Jobs

❶ 医者
isha

❷ 配管工
haikankoh

❸ 店主
tenshu

❹ 会計士
kaikehshi

❺ 学生
gakusei

❻ 弁護士
bengoshi

2 Jobs (3 minutes)

What are these jobs in Japanese?

❶ doctor

❷ plumber

❸ retailer

❹ accountant

❺ student

❻ lawyer

clock ❼

3 Work (4 minutes)

Answer these questions following the English prompts.

goshokugyoh wa
❶ Say "I'm a dentist."

doko no kaisha ni otsutome desuka
❷ Say "I'm self-employed."

doko de oshiete irasshai masuka
❸ Say "I teach at Tokyo University."

moshi moshi
❹ Say "I'd like to arrange an appointment."

3 Work

❶ 歯医者です。
ha-isha desu

❷ 自営業です。
ji-eigyoh desu

❸ 東京大学です。
Tokyo daigaku desu

❹ アポを取りたいの
ですが。
apo o toritai no desuga

4 How much? (4 minutes)

Answer the question with the price shown in parentheses.

❶ *koh-hi wa ikura desuka*
(¥300)

❷ *heya wa ikura desuka*
(¥8,000)

❸ *pasokon wa ikura desuka* (¥100,000)

❹ *chiketto wa ikura desuka* (¥700)

4 How much?

❶ 三百円です。
san byaku yen desu

❷ 八千円です。
hassen yen desu

❸ 十万円です。
jyu-man yen desu

❹ 七百円です。
nana hyaku yen desu

1 Warm up (1 minute)

Say "Can you give me the receipt?" (pp.68-69)

Ask "Do you have any cakes?" (pp.18-19)

YAKKYOKU DE
At the pharmacy

To describe an ailment, you can use the phrase *...ga shimasu* (I have ...)—for example, *zutsu ga shimasu* (I have a headache), or you could say *...ga itai desu* (I have a pain in my ...). Notice that the ailment or part of the body comes first in the sentence.

2 Match and repeat (3 minutes)

Match the numbered items to the Japanese words in the panel below and test yourself using the cover flap.

❶ 包帯
hohtai

❷ シロップ
shiroppu

❸ 目薬
megusuri

❹ 軟膏
nankoh

❺ 絆創膏
bansohkoh

❻ 注射器
chu-sha ki

❼ 座薬
zayaku

❽ 錠剤
jyohzai

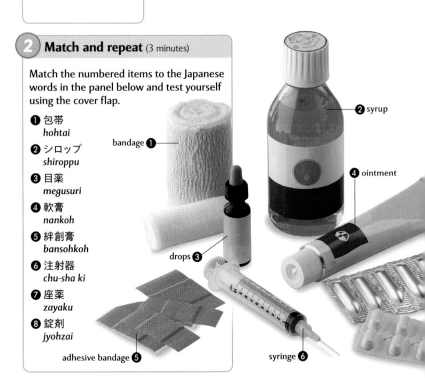

bandage ❶

❷ syrup

❹ ointment

drops ❸

adhesive bandage ❺

syringe ❻

3 In conversation (3 minutes)

こんにちは。
どうしましたか?
konnichiwa.
doh shimashitaka

Hello. What's the matter?

腹痛がします。
fukutsu ga shimasu

I have a stomachache.

下痢気味ですか?
geri gimi desuka

Do you also have diarrhea?

4 Words to remember (2 minutes)

Familiarize yourself with these words and test yourself using the flap.

頭痛がします。
zutsu ga shimasu
I have a headache.

headache	頭痛 *zutsu*
stomachache	腹痛 *fukutsu*
diarrhea	下痢 *geri*
cold	風邪 *kaze*
cough	せき *seki*
sunburn	日焼け *hiyake*
toothache	歯痛 *ha-ita*

5 Say it (2 minutes)

I have a toothache.

I have a cough.

Do you have that as an ointment?

7 suppository

8 tablet

6 Useful phrases (4 minutes)

Learn these phrases and then test yourself using the cover flap.

I have a pain in my leg.	脚が痛いです。 *ashi ga itai desu*
Do you have that as a syrup?	それのシロップは ありますか? *sore no shiroppu wa arimasuka*
I'm allergic to penicillin.	ペニシリンに対して アレルギー体質です。 *penishirin ni taishite arerugih taishitsu desu*

いいえ、でも頭痛 がします。
ihe, demo zutsu ga shimasu

No, but I have a headache.

これをお飲み下さい。
kore o onomi kudasai

Take this.

それの錠剤は ありますか?
sore no jyohzai wa arimasuka

Do you have that as tablets?

KARADA
The body

Say "I have a toothache" and "I have a pain in my leg." (pp.88–89)

Ask politely "What's the matter?" (pp.88–89)

Spoken Japanese uses the same pronunciation for leg and foot: *ashi*. However, the written characters are different. There are two separate words describing the back area: *lower back* is **koshi**; *upper back* is **senaka**. Remember there is no plural, so **meh** is *eye* or *eyes*.

2 **Match and repeat: body** (6 minutes)

Match the numbered parts of the body with the list below. Test yourself by using the cover flap.

❶ 手
te

❷ 頭
atama

❸ 肩
kata

❹ 肘
hiji

❺ 髪
kami

❻ 腕
ude

❼ 首
kubi

❽ 胸
mune

❾ お腹
onaka

❿ 脚
ashi

⓫ 膝
hiza

⓬ 足
ashi

hand ❶
head ❷
shoulder ❸
❹ elbow
❺ hair
❻ arm
❼ neck
❽ chest
❾ stomach
❿ leg
⓫ knee
⓬ foot

3 Match and repeat: face (3 minutes)

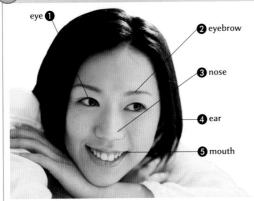

eye ❶

❷ eyebrow

❸ nose

❹ ear

❺ mouth

Match the numbered facial features with the list below.

❶ 目
meh

❷ 眉
mayu

❸ 鼻
hana

❹ 耳
mimi

❺ 口
kuchi

4 Useful phrases (3 minutes)

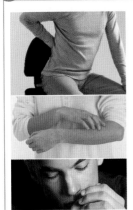

Learn these phrases and then test yourself using the cover flap.

I have a pain in my lower back.	腰が痛いです。 *koshi ga itai desu*	

I have a rash on my arm. 　腕がかぶれています。 *ude ga kaburete imasu*

I don't feel well. 　調子が悪いです。 *chohshi ga warui desu*

5 Put into practice (2 minutes)

Join in this conversation and test yourself using the cover flap.

どうしました?　調子が悪いです。
doh shimashita　*chohshi ga warui desu*

What's the matter?

Say: I don't feel well.

どこが痛みますか?　肩が痛いです。
doko ga itami masuka　*kata ga itai desu*

Where does it hurt?

Say: I have a pain in my shoulder.

1 Warm up (1 minute)

Say "I have a headache."
(pp.88-89)

Now, say "I have a pain
in my ear." (pp.90-91)

Ask "What's the matter?"
(pp.88-89)

ISHA TO
With the doctor

Most Japanese doctors are based in hospitals rather
than in separate clinics. You will usually need to go
to a hospital for an appointment, even for minor
ailments. Many Japanese doctors speak good English,
but you could need to give a basic explanation in
Japanese, for example, to a receptionist.

2 Useful phrases you may hear (3 minutes)

Learn these phrases and then test yourself
using the cover flap to conceal the Japanese
on the left.

今飲んでいる薬は
ありますか?
*ima nondeiru kusuri
wa arimasuka*
Are you taking any medication?

大したことはありません。 *taishitakoto wa arimasen*	It's not serious.
検査が必要です。 *kensa ga hitsuyoh desu*	Tests are needed.
骨折です。 *kossetsu desu*	You have a fracture.
入院が必要です。 *nyu-in ga hitsuyoh desu*	You need to stay in the hospital. (Literally: hospital is needed.)

3 In conversation (5 minutes)

どうしましたか?
doh shimashitaka

What's the matter?

胸が痛いです。
mune ga itai desu

I have a pain in my chest.

診察しましょう。
shinsatsu shimashoh

I'll need to examine you.

4 Useful phrases you may need to say (4 minutes)

Learn these phrases and then test yourself using the cover flap.

I'm diabetic.	糖尿病です。	*tohnyoh byoh desu*
I'm epileptic.	てんかん持ちです。	*tenkan mochi desu*
I'm asthmatic.	ぜんそく持ちです。	*zensoku mochi desu*
I have a heart condition.	心臓が弱いです。	*shinzoh ga yowai desu*
I have a fever.	熱があります。	*netsu ga arimasu*
It's urgent.	緊急です。	*kinkyu desu*
I feel breathless.	息が苦しいです。	*iki ga kurushih desu*

妊娠しています。
ninshin shite imasu
I'm pregnant.

Cultural tip

There are two separate emergency numbers in Japan depending on which service you require. For the police, dial 110; for ambulance and fire service, dial 119.

5 Say it (2 minutes)

I have a pain in my arm.

Is it urgent?

重い病気ですか?
omoi byohki desuka

Is it serious?

いいえ、ただの消化不良です。
ihe, tadano shohka furyoh desu

No, you only have indigestion.

よかった! 安心しました。
yokatta. anshin shimashita

Good! What a relief.

BYOH-IN DE
In the hospital

It is useful to know a few basic Japanese phrases relating to hospitals for use in an emergency or in case you need to visit a friend or colleague in the hospital. Japanese medical care is excellent but very expensive, so make sure you have adequate insurance.

1 **Warm up** (1 minute)

Say "Where's the florist?" (pp.68-69)

Say "Tests are needed." (pp.92-93)

What is the Japanese for "mouth" and "head"? (pp.90-91)

2 **Useful phrases** (5 minutes)

Familiarize yourself with these phrases. Conceal the Japanese with the cover flap and test yourself.

待合室はどこ ですか? *machiai shitsu wa doko desuka*	Where's the waiting room?
どのくらいかかり ますか? *dono kurai kakari masuka*	How long does it take?
痛いですか? *itai desuka*	Will it hurt?
ベッドに横になって ください。 *beddo ni yoko ni natte kudasai*	Please lie down on the bed.
六時間何も食べないで ください *roku jikan nanimo tabenaide kudasai*	Please do not eat anything for six hours.
頭を動かさないで ください。 *atama o ugokasanai de kudasai*	Don't move your head.
口を開けて ください。 *kuchi o akete kudasai*	Open your mouth.
血液検査が必要 です。 *ketsueki kensa ga hitsuyoh desu*	A blood test is needed.

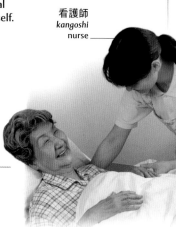

看護師
kangoshi
nurse

具合はいいですか?
guai wa iidesuka
Are you feeling better?

訪問時間はいつですか?
hohmon jikan wa itsu desuka
What are the visiting hours?

3 Words to remember (4 minutes)

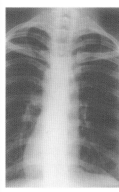

Memorize these words and test yourself using the cover flap.

emergency ward	緊急病棟 *kinkyu byohtoh*
children's ward	小児病棟 *shohni byohtoh*
operating room	手術室 *shujyutsu shitsu*
waiting room	待合室 *machiai shitsu*
corridor	廊下 *rohka*
stairs	階段 *kaidan*
elevator	エレベーター *erebehtah*

レントゲンは正常です。
rentogen wa seijyoh desu
The x-ray is normal.

4 Put into practice (3 minutes)

Join in this conversation. Read the Japanese on the left and follow the instructions to make your reply. Then test yourself by hiding the answers with the cover flap.

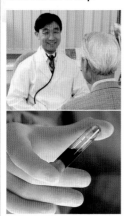

大したことは
ありません。
taishitakoto wa arimasen

It's not serious.

Ask: Are tests needed?

検査が必要ですか?
kensa ga hitsuyoh desuka

血液検査が必要
です。
*ketsueki kensa ga
hitsuyoh desu*

A blood test is needed.

Ask: Will it hurt?

痛いですか?
itai desuka

5 Say it (2 minutes)

Is a blood test needed?

Where's the children's ward?

An x-ray is needed.

Read it It's useful to be able to recognize the Japanese for *hospital*. This literally means *sick building*. The first character 病 *byoh* can also be found in other words such as 病気 *byoh-ki*, *sickness*, and 病人 *byoh-nin*, *sick person* or *patient*.

病院 *byoh-in* *hospital*

Kotae
Answers (Cover with flap)

FUKUSHU TO KURIKAESHI
Review and repeat

1 The body

❶ 頭
atama

❷ 腕
ude

❸ 胸
mune

❹ お腹
onaka

❺ 脚
ashi

❻ 膝
hiza

❼ 足
ashi

1 The body (4 minutes)

Name the numbered body parts in Japanese.

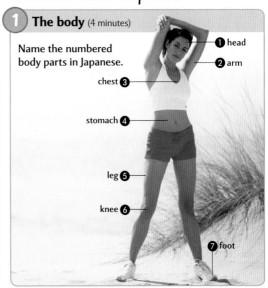

- **❶** head
- **❷** arm
- chest **❸**
- stomach **❹**
- leg **❺**
- knee **❻**
- **❼** foot

2 On the phone

❶ 大和さんお願いします。
Yamato-san onegai shimasu

❷ ゴープレス・プリンターのジャック・ハントと申します。
Gopress purintah no Jack Hunt to mohshimasu

❸ メッセージを伝えていただけますか？
messehji o tsutaete itadake masuka

❹ ミーティングは火曜日ではありません。
mihtingu wa kayoh bi dewa arimasen

❺ ありがとうございます。
arigatoh gozaimasu

2 On the phone (4 minutes)

You are arranging an appointment. Follow the conversation, replying in Japanese with the help of the numbered English prompts.

moshi moshi, japanihzu konekushon desu
❶ I'd like to speak to Mr. Yamato.

dochira sama desuka
❷ Jack Hunt of Gopress Printers.

sumimasenga, ima hanashichu desu
❸ Can I leave a message?

mochiron desu
❹ The meeting isn't on Tuesday.

wakarimashita
❺ Thank you very much.

3 Clothing (3 minutes)

Say the Japanese words for the numbered items of clothing.

- ❶ jacket
- tie ❷
- ❻ skirt
- pants ❸
- ❺ pantyhose
- shoes ❹

3 Clothing

❶ ジャケット
jyaketto

❷ ネクタイ
nekutai

❸ パンツ
pantsu

❹ 靴
kutsu

❺ ストッキング
sutokkingu

❻ スカート
sukahto

4 At the doctor (4 minutes)

Say these phrases in Japanese.

❶ I have a pain in my leg.

❷ Is it serious?

❸ I have a heart condition.

❹ Will it hurt?

❺ I'm pregnant.

4 At the doctor

❶ 脚が痛いです。
ashi ga itai desu

❷ 重い病気ですか？
omoi byohki desuka

❸ 心臓が弱いです。
shinzoh ga yowai desu

❹ 痛いですか？
itai desuka

❺ 妊娠しています。
ninshin shite imasu

IE
Home

In Japan, space is limited, and most city dwellers live in *apartments* (*aparto* or the more luxurious **manshon**). Rooms are often small, and a *combined kitchen and dining room* (*dainingu kitchin*) is common. Earthquakes are frequent, and buildings have to comply with strict specifications.

1 Warm up (1 minute)

Say the months of the year in Japanese. (pp.28-29)

Ask "Is there a museum in town?" (pp.48-49) and "How much is that?" (pp.18-19)

2 Match and repeat (5 minutes)

Match the numbered items to the list and test yourself using the flap.

❶ 雨どい
amadoi

❷ バルコニー
barukonih

❸ 窓
mado

❹ 雨戸
amado

❺ 屋根
yane

❻ 壁
kabe

❼ ドア
doa

❽ 階段
kaidan

❾ 庭
niwa

❶ gutter　❷ balcony　❸ window　shutter ❹

garden ❾　steps ❽　door ❼

Cultural tip In addition to being built to withstand earthquakes, most Japanese buildings have steel or wooden anti-typhoon shutters. These can be closed quickly to seal off the house or apartment from raging winds and rain. The hurricane and typhoon season lasts from late August to early October, although storms can occur outside these months.

3 Words to remember (4 minutes)

家賃は一月いくら
ですか?
yachin wa hitotsuki ikura desuka
How much is the rent per month?

5 roof

Familiarize yourself with these words and
test yourself using the flap.

room	部屋 *heya*
floor	床 *yuka*
ceiling	天井 *ten-jyoh*
bedroom	寝室 *shinshitsu*
bathroom	バスルーム *basu ru-mu*
kitchen	台所 *daidokoro*
dining room	ダイニングルーム *dainingu ru-mu*
living room	居間 *ima*
attic	屋根裏 *yane ura*
parking space	車庫 *shako*

wall **6**

4 Useful phrases (3 minutes)

Learn these phrases and test yourself.

車庫はありますか?
shako wa arimasuka

Is there a parking space?

いつ入居できますか?
itsu nyu-kyo dekimasuka

When can I move in?

家具付きですか?
kagu tsuki desuka

Is it furnished?

5 Say it (2 minutes)

Is there a dining room?

Where's the attic?

It's furnished.

IE NO NAKA DE
Inside the home

1 Warm up (1 minute)

What's the Japanese for "table" (pp.20-21), "desk" (pp.80-81), "bed" (pp.60-61), and "curtains" (pp.60-61)?

How do you say "This car is small"? (pp.64-65)

The Japanese often end their sentences with short "markers" that don't really change the meaning but carry different nuances. For example, the **yo** marker can imply *and even* or *to be sure* and **ne** can mean something like *isn't that so?* You'll see examples of these in the conversation below.

2 Match and repeat (3 minutes)

Match the numbered items to the list in the panel below. Then test yourself by concealing the Japanese with the cover flap.

❶ 流し
nagashi

❷ 蛇口
jyaguchi

❸ 炊飯器
sui-hanki

❹ 調理台
chohridai

❺ 食器洗い機
shokki araiki

❻ 椅子
isu

❼ 戸棚
todana

❽ テーブル
tehburu

faucet ❷

❶ sink

rice cooker ❸

❺ dishwasher   chair ❻   ❼ cabinet   table ❽

3 In conversation (3 minutes)

これが冷蔵庫です。
kore ga reizohko desu

This is the refrigerator.

炊飯器はありますか?
sui-hanki wa arimasuka

Is there a rice cooker?

はい、そしてこれが
レンジです。
hai, soshite kore ga renji desu

Yes, and here's the stove.

4 Words to remember (2 minutes)

Familiarize yourself with these words and test yourself using the flap.

このソファは新しいです。
kono sofa wa atarashih desu
This couch is new.

couch	ソファ *sofa*
carpet	絨毯 *jyu-tan*
bath	バス *basu*
toilet	トイレ *to-ee-reh*
stove	レンジ *renji*
washing machine	洗濯機 *sentaku ki*
refrigerator	冷蔵庫 *reizohko*

4 counter

6 Say it (2 minutes)

Is there a washing machine?

The refrigerator is new.

The faucet is broken.

5 Useful phrases (4 minutes)

Learn these phrases and then test yourself using the cover flap to conceal the Japanese.

The refrigerator is broken.	冷蔵庫が壊れています。 *reizohko ga kowarete imasu*
I'm not fond of the curtains.	カーテンが気に入りません。 *kahten ga kini irimasen*
Are heat and electricity included?	光熱費込みですか? *kohnetsu hi komi desuka*

流しが新しいですね。
nagashi ga atarashih desune
The sink is new.

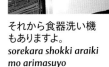
それから食器洗い機もありますよ。
sorekara shokki araiki mo arimasuyo
And there's even a dishwasher.

なんてきれいなタイルなんでしょう!
nante kireh na tairu nandeshoh
What pretty tiles!

1 Warm up (1 minute)

What's the Japanese for "day" and "month"? (pp.28-29)

Say "Where's the florist?" (pp.68-69) and "Is there a garden?" (pp.98-99)

NIWA
The garden

Japanese gardens, often with water features and plants like lilies and cherry trees, can be seen in public places such as parks, temples, and hotels. Space constraints mean that many Japanese homes don't have their own gardens, but houseplants and flower arrangements are popular.

2 Words to remember (3 minutes)

Familiarize yourself with these words and test yourself using the flap.

冬 *fuyu*	winter	
春 *haru*	spring	
夏 *natsu*	summer	
秋 *aki*	fall	

❷ tree

plants ❸

waterfall ❶

flowers ❿

stones ❾

rocks ❽

3 Useful phrases (4 minutes)

Learn these phrases and then test yourself using the cover flap.

What kind of tree is this?	これは何の木ですか? *kore wa nanno ki desuka*
I like the pond.	池が好きです。 *ike ga suki desu*
What beautiful flowers!	きれいな花ですね! *kireh na hana desune*
Can we walk in the garden?	庭を歩いていいですか? *niwa o aruite ihdesuka*

4 Match and repeat (5 minutes)

soil **4**

5 path

6 grass

7 pond

Match the numbered items to the words in the panel below.

1 滝
taki

2 木
ki

3 植物
shokubutsu

4 土
tsuchi

5 小道
komichi

6 草
kusa

7 池
ike

8 岩
iwa

9 石
ishi

10 花
hana

5 Say it (2 minutes)

What kind of flower is this?

I like the waterfall.

Is there a pond?

DOHBUTSU
Animals

Say "My name is John."
(pp.8-9)

Say "I like the pond."
(pp.102-103)

What's "fish" in Japanese?
(pp.22-23)

The Japanese tend to keep small lap dogs and sometimes cats in the house as pets. There is not usually enough space indoors for larger animals. Reptiles and insects, such as snakes and crickets, are also popular, particularly among young boys.

2 Match and repeat (3 minutes)

Match the numbered animals to the Japanese words in the panel below. Then test yourself using the cover flap.

❶ 猫
neko

❷ 鳥
tori

❸ 魚
sakana

❹ 犬
inu

❺ 馬
uma

bird ❷

cat ❶

fish ❸

dog ❹

❺ horse

3 Useful phrases (4 minutes)

Learn these phrases and then test yourself using the cover flap.

この犬はおとなしいですか? *kono inu wa otonashih desuka*	Is this dog friendly?
名前は何ですか? *namae wa nandesuka*	What's his name?
猫は苦手です。 *neko wa negate desu*	I don't really care for cats.
この犬は噛み付きませんよ。 *kono inu wa kamitsuki masenyo*	This dog doesn't bite.

あなたの猫ですか?
anata no neko desuka
Is this your cat?

Cultural tip Some buildings will keep larger dogs outside as guard dogs. Native Japanese dog breeds, such as the Kishuken, Shibaken, and Ainuken, are known for their toughness and are employed as "yard" dogs rather than treated as pets.

猛犬に注意
Beware of the Dog

あれは何という魚
ですか?
a-re wa nanto yu sakana desuka
What's that fish called?

4 Words to remember (4 minutes)

Familiarize yourself with these words and test yourself using the flap.

monkey	猿	*saru*
sheep	羊	*hitsuji*
cow	牛	*ushi*
pig	豚	*buta*
rabbit	兎	*usagi*
mouse	ネズミ	*nezumi*

Read it Most basic words referring to natural features or animals, such as *tree*, *dog*, *flower*, *cow*, etc., are written in *kanji*—often with just a single character. Look at the *kanji* for animals on this page and see if you can spot them in the example phrases.

5 Put into practice (3 minutes)

Join in this conversation. Read the Japanese on the left and follow the instructions to make your reply. Then test yourself by concealing the answers with the cover flap.

あなたの犬ですか?
anata no inu desuka

Is this your dog?

Say: Yes, his name is Ichiroh.

はい、イチローと
います。
hai, Ichiroh to ihmasu

犬は苦手です。
inu wa negate desu

I don't really care for dogs.

Say: Don't worry. He's friendly.

大丈夫です。
おとなしいですよ。
daijyohbu desu.
otonashih desu yo.

FUKUSHU TO KURIKAESHI
Review and repeat

1 Colors

❶ 白
shiro

❷ 黄色
ki iro

❸ 緑
midori

❹ 黒
kuro

❺ 赤
aka

❻ 青
ao

❼ ピンク
pinku

1 Colors (4 minutes)

What are these colors in Japanese?

❶ white
❷ yellow
❸ green
❹ black
❺ red
❻ blue
❼ pink

2 Kitchen

❶ 調理台
chohridai

❷ 流し
nagashi

❸ 蛇口
jyaguchi

❹ 炊飯器
sui-hanki

❺ 食器洗い機
shokki araiki

❻ 椅子
isu

❼ 戸棚
todana

❽ テーブル
tehburu

2 Kitchen (4 minutes)

Say the Japanese words for the numbered items.

counter ❶ sink ❷ ❸ faucet rice ❹ cooker dishwasher ❺ chair ❻ cabinet ❼

3 House (4 minutes)

You are visiting a house in Japan. Join in the conversation, replying in Japanese where you see the numbered English prompts.

basu ru-mu wa kochira desu
❶ What pretty tiles!

daidokoro wa ohkih desu
❷ Is there a washing machine?

hai, sorekara shokki araiki mo arimasuyo
❸ Is there a parking space?

ihe demo niwa ga arimasu
❹ Is it furnished?

mochiron desu
❺ How much is the rent per month?

3 House

❶ なんてきれいな
タイルなん
でしょう！
nante kireh na tairu nandeshoh

❷ 洗濯機は
ありますか？
sentaku ki wa arimasuka

❸ 車庫はありますか？
shako wa arimasuka

❹ 家具付きですか？
kagu tsuki desuka

❺ 家賃は一月いくらで
すか？
yachin wa hitotsuki ikura desuka

4 At home (3 minutes)

Say the Japanese for the following items.

❶ washing machine
❷ couch
❸ attic
❹ dining room
❺ tree
❻ garden

❽ table

4 At home

❶ 洗濯機
sentaku ki

❷ ソファ
sofa

❸ 屋根裏
yane ura

❹ ダイニング
ルーム
dainingu ru-mu

❺ 木
ki

❻ 庭
niwa

1 Warm up (1 minute)

Ask "How do I get to the station?" and "Where's the post office?" (pp.50-51 and pp.68-69)

What's the Japanese for passport? (pp.54-55)

Ask "What time is it?" (pp.30-31)

Postcards are a popular form of letter in Japan, especially when sending a New Year's greeting. Some postcards are prepaid (the bird and flower pictures work as stamps), so you can mail them as soon as you write them.

2 Words to remember: mail (3 minutes)

手紙 *tegami*	letter
封筒 *fu-toh*	envelope
小包 *kozutsumi*	package
エアメール *ea mehru*	air mail
書留郵便 *kakitome yu-bin*	registered mail
切手 *kitte*	stamps
郵便配達人 *yu-bin haitatsu nin*	mail carrier
ポスト *posuto*	mailbox

Familiarize yourself with these words and test yourself using the cover flap to conceal the Japanese on the left.

はがき
hagaki
postcard

3 In conversation (3 minutes)

お金を両替したいです。
okane o ryohgae shitai desu

I'd like to change some money.

身分証明書をお持ちですか?
mibun shohmehsho o omochi desuka

Do you have any identification?

はい、これがパスポートです。
hai, kore ga pasupohto desu

Yes, here's my passport.

クレジットカード
kurejitto kahdo
credit card

クレジットカードで
払えますか?
kurejitto kahdo de harae masuka
Can I pay with a credit card?

4 Words to remember: bank (2 minutes)

Familiarize yourself with these words and test yourself
using the cover flap to conceal the Japanese on the right.

money	お金 *okane*
PIN	ピン、暗証番号 *pin 、ansho bangoh*
cashier	窓口 *madoguchi*
bills	紙幣 *shiheh*
coins	硬貨 *kohka*
ATM	ATM *"ATM"*
exchange rate	レート *rehto*

5 Useful phrases (4 minutes)

Learn these phrases and then test yourself using
the cover flap.

I'd like to change some money.	お金を両替したいです。 *okane o ryohgae shitai desu*
What is the exchange rate?	レートはいくらですか? *rehto wa ikura desuka*
Where's the ATM?	ATMはどこですか? *"ATM" wa doko desuka*

6 Say it (2 minutes)

I'd like to change
some dollars.

Here's my credit card.

Where's the mailbox?

ここにご署名をお願いします。
koko ni goshomeh o onegai shimasu

Please sign here.

どんな紙幣をご希望ですか?
donna shihei o gokiboh desuka

How would you like
the bills?

五千円札をお願い
します。
go-sen-yen satsu o onegai shimasu

5,000-yen bills, please.

1 **Warm up** (1 minute)

What is the Japanese for "The refrigerator is broken"? (pp.100–101)

What's the Japanese for "today" and "tomorrow"? (pp.28–29)

Say "Thank you very much." (pp.40–41)

SHU-RI
Repairs

You can combine the Japanese words on these pages with the vocabulary you learned in week 10 to help you explain basic problems and cope with arranging most repairs. Rented accommodations are usually arranged via *agents*, known as **fudohsanya**. They can also help with problems.

2 **Words to remember** (4 minutes)

Familiarize yourself with these words and test yourself using the flap.

配管工 *haikankoh*	plumber
電気技師 *denki gishi*	electrician
機械技師 *kikai gishi*	mechanic
建築家 *kenchiku ka*	builder
大工 *daiku*	carpenter
コンピューター修理店 *konpyu-tah shu-ri ten*	computer repair store
清掃業者 *seisoh gyohsha*	cleaner
コック *kokku*	cook

機械技師は必要ないです。
kikai gishi wa hitsuyoh nai desu
I don't need a mechanic.

3 **In conversation** (3 minutes)

おはようございます。
山田ですが。
ohayoh gozaimasu.
Yamada desuga

Good morning.
This is Mrs. Yamada.

おはようございます。
どうかなさいましたか?
ohayoh gozaimasu.
dohka nasai mashitaka

Good morning. Is there anything wrong?

食器洗い機が壊れています。
shokki araiki ga kowarete imasu

The dishwasher is broken.

4 Useful phrases (3 minutes)

これはどこで修理してもら
えますか?
*kore wa doko de shu-ri shite
mora-e masuka*
Where can I get this repaired?

Learn these phrases and then test yourself using
the cover flap.

Please clean the bathroom.	バスルームを掃除してください。 *basu ru-mu o sohji shite kudasai*
Can you repair the television?	テレビを修理してもらえますか? *terebi o shu-ri shite mora-e masuka*
Can you recommend a good mechanic?	良い修理屋を紹介してもらえますか? *ih shu-ri ya o shohkai shite mora-e masuka*

5 Put into practice (4 minutes)

今日中に修理できる
でしょう。
kyohjyu-ni shu-ri dekiru deshoh
It's possible to repair it today.

Cover up the text on the right and complete the
dialogue in Japanese.

CDドライブが壊れています。
CD doraibu ga kowarete imasu

Your CD drive is broken.

Ask: Can you recommend a
good computer repair store?

良いコンピューター修理店
を紹介してもらえますか?
ih konpyu-tah shu-ri ten o shohkai shite mora-e masuka

街に一店あります。
machi ni itten arimasu

There's one in town.

Say: Thank you very much.

どうもありがとう
ございます。
dohmo arigatoh gozaimasu

修理担当者を送ります。
*shu-ri tantoh sha
o okuri masu*

We'll send a repairman.

今日中に来てくれ
ますか?
kyohjyu ni kite kure masuka

Can you do it today?

すみません。明日の朝に
なります。
*sumimasen. ashita no asa
ni narimasu*

Sorry. But it will be
tomorrow morning.

Say the days of the week in Japanese. (pp.28-29)

How do you say "cleaner"? (pp.110-111)

Say "It's 9:30," "10:45," and "12:00." (pp.30-31)

KURU
To come

Japanese verbs don't generally change with the subject but do take different endings according to the tense or "mood" (see pp.40-41). Below you will see some of these changes for the verb *kuru* (to come) with examples, including the useful *ki-te* form used for invitations.

2 Useful phrases (6 minutes)

Say the different forms of *kuru* (to come) aloud. Use the cover flap to test yourself and, when you are confident, practice the sample sentences below.

来る *kuru*	to come (infinitive)
来ます *kimasu*	come/coming (present)
来ません *kimasen*	not come/coming (present negative)
来ました *kimashita*	came (past)
来ませんでした *kimasen deshita*	didn't come (past negative)
来て *ki-te*	come! (invitation)
バスが来ません。 *basu ga kimasen*	The bus isn't coming.
大工さんは九時に来ました。 *daikusan wa kuji ni kimashita*	The carpenter came at nine o'clock.
清掃業者は今日は来ませんでした。 *sehsoh gyohsha wa kyoh wa kimasen deshita*	The cleaner didn't come today.
明日来るつもりです。 *ashita kuru tsumori desu*	I intend to come tomorrow.

彼らは電車で来ます。
karera wa densha de kimasu
They're coming by train.

Conversational tip Beware of English phrases using *come* that translate differently in Japanese. For example, the Japanese equivalent of *I come from Australia* would be **ohsutoraria jin desu**, which translates literally as *Australia person I am.*

3 Invitations (4 minutes)

You can use *ki-te* (come!) with *kudasai* (please) for basic invitations, but there are also different expressions depending on the level of formality.

Please come to my birthday party.	私の誕生パーティーに来てください。 *watashi no tanjyoh pahtih ni ki-te kudasai*
Can you come to our reception on Monday? (formal)	月曜日のレセプションにいらしていただけますか? *getsuyoh-bi no resepushon ni irashite itadake masuka*
Would you be able to come to our seminar on Friday? (very formal)	金曜日のセミナーにお越し願えますでしょうか? *kinyoh-bi no seminah ni okoshi negaemasu deshohka*
Come to my dinner party! (informal)	ディナーパーティーに来てね! *dinah pahtih ni kitene*

4 Put into practice (4 minutes)

Join in this conversation. Read the Japanese on the left and follow the instructions to make your reply. Then test yourself by concealing the answers with the cover flap.

もしもし。 *moshi moshi* Hello. Say: Hello. Please come to my birthday party.	もしもし。私の誕生パーティーに来てください。 *moshi moshi. watashi no tanjyoh pahtih ni ki-te kudasai*
パーティーはいつですか? *pahtih wa itsu desuka* When is the party? Say: It's tomorrow at eight o'clock.	明日の8時です。 *ashitano hachi ji desu*
はい、ぜひ。 *hai, zehi* Yes, I'd love to. Say: So see you tomorrow.	ではまたあした。 *dewa mata ashita*

KEHSATSU TO HANZAI
Police and crime

1 Warm up (1 minute)

What's the Japanese for "tall" and "short"? (pp.64-65)

Say "The room is big" and "The bed is small." (pp.64-65)

Japanese police cars are black and white with a red strip light on the roof. The uniforms are blue and gray with a peaked cap. Note that the terms *otoko* (man) and *onna* (woman) in section 4 are not very polite as they refer to criminal suspects. More polite equivalents would be *danseh* and *jyoseh*.

2 Words to remember: crime (4 minutes)

Familiarize yourself with these words.

どろぼう *doroboh*	thief/burglar
通報 *tsuh-hoh*	police report
報告書 *hohkoku sho*	statement
証人 *shoh nin*	witness
目撃者 *mokugeki sha*	eyewitness
弁護士 *bengo shi*	lawyer
警察官 *kehsatsu kan*	police officer

弁護士が必要です。
bengo shi ga hitsuyoh desu
I need a lawyer.

3 Useful phrases (3 minutes)

Learn these phrases and then test yourself using the cover flap.

すられました。 *surare mashita*	I've been pickpocketed.
何が盗まれましたか? *nani ga nusumare mashitaka*	What was stolen?
犯人を見ましたか? *hannin o mimashitaka*	Did you see who did it?
いつおこりましたか? *itsu okori mashitaka*	When did it happen?

カメラ
kamera
camera

お金
okane
money

財布
saifu
wallet

4 Words to remember: appearance (5 minutes)

Learn these words and then test yourself using the cover flap.

男は白髪混じりで眼鏡をかけていました。
otoko wa shiraga majiri de megane o kakete imashita
The man had gray hair and glasses.

女は背が高く髪が長かったです。
onna wa se ga takaku kami ga nagakatta desu
The woman was tall and had long hair.

man/men	男 *otoko*
woman/women	女 *onna*
tall	背の高い *se no takai*
short	背の低い *se no hikui*
young	若い *wakai*
old	年を取った *toshi o totta*
fat	太った *futotta*
thin	痩せた *yaseta*
beard	あごひげ *ago hige*
mustache	口ひげ *kuchi hige*
glasses	眼鏡 *megane*

Read it The Japanese script for *police* is written with two *kanji* characters: 警察 (*kehsatsu*). Adding the character 官 (*kan*) will produce *policeman*: 警察官 (*kehsatsu kan*); and adding 署 (*sho*) will produce *police station*: 警察署 (*kehsatsu sho*).

5 Put into practice (2 minutes)

Practice these phrases. Then use the cover flap to hide the text on the right and follow the instructions to make your reply in Japanese.

男はどんな格好でしたか？
otoko wa donna kakkoh deshita ka

Can you describe him?

Say: He was short and fat.

背が低く太っていました。
se ga hikuku futotte imashita

髪は？
kami wa

And the hair?

Say: He had gray hair and a beard.

白髪であごひげを生やしていました。
shiraga de ago hige o hayashite imashita

Kotae
Answers (Cover with flap)

FUKUSHU TO KURIKAESHI
Review and repeat

1 To come

❶ 私はバスで来ます。
watashi wa basu de kimasu

❷ 電気技師は昨日来ました。
denki gishi wa kinoh kimashita

❸ 私の誕生パーティーに来てください。
watashi no tanjyoh pahtih ni ki-te kudasai

❹ 清掃業者は木曜日には来ませんでした。
sehsoh gyohsha wa mokuyoh bi niwa kimasen deshita

1 To come (3 minutes)

Put the following sentences into Japanese using the correct form of *kuru* (to come).

❶ I'm coming by bus.

❷ The electrician came yesterday.

❸ Please come to my birthday party.

❹ The cleaner didn't come on Thursday.

2 Bank and mail

❶ クレジットカード
kurejitto kahdo

❷ 紙幣
shiheh

❸ はがき
hagaki

❹ 小包
kozutsumi

❺ 切手
kitte

2 Bank and mail (4 minutes)

Name the numbered items in Japanese.

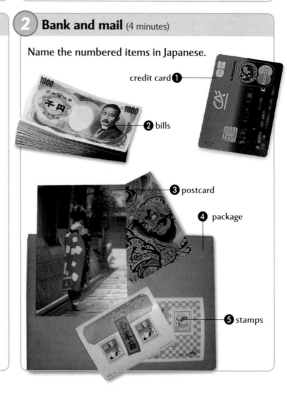

credit card ❶

❷ bills

❸ postcard

❹ package

❺ stamps

3 Appearance (4 minutes)

What do these descriptions mean?

❶ *se ga hikuku yasete imashita*

❷ *otoko wa shohto katto deshita*

❸ *onna wa megane o kakete imashita*

❹ *otoko wa kuchi hige o hayashite imashita*

❺ *otoko wa shiraga de ago hige o hayashite imashita*

3 Appearance

❶ He was short and thin.

❷ The man had short hair.

❸ The woman had glasses.

❹ The man had a mustache.

❺ He had gray hair and a beard.

4 The pharmacy (4 minutes)

You are asking a pharmacist for advice. Join in the conversation, replying in Japanese where you see the numbered English prompts.

konnichiwa. doh shimashitaka
❶ I have a stomachache.

kaze gimi desuka
❷ No, but I have a headache.

kore o onomi kudasai
❸ Do you have that as a syrup?

hai, arimasu
❹ How much is that?

happyaku yen ni narimasu
❺ Thank you.

4 The pharmacy

❶ 腹痛がします。
fukutsu ga shimasu

❷ いいえ、でも
頭痛がします。
ihe, demo zutsu ga shimasu

❸ それのシロップは
ありますか？
sore no shiroppu wa arimasuka

❹ いくらですか？
ikura desuka

❺ ありがとう。
arigatoh

REJYAH
Leisure time

1 **Warm up** (1 minute)

What is the Japanese for "museum" and "movie theater"? (pp.48-49)

Say "I like the pond." (p.103)

Ask "What's your profession?" (pp.78-79)

Popular leisure activities outside the house include shopping, playing in the ubiquitous and often very large arcades, or going to karaoke "boxes." New theme parks open regularly and are popular with adults and children alike. Sumo is popular with older people, but theater and opera are minority pursuits.

2 **Words to remember** (4 minutes)

Familiarize yourself with these words and test yourself using the cover flap to conceal the Japanese on the left.

劇場 *gekijyoh*	theater
映画 *eiga*	movies/film
テーマパーク *tehma pahku*	theme park
音楽 *ongaku*	music
アート *ahto*	art
スポーツ *supohtsu*	sports
旅行 *ryokoh*	traveling
読書 *dokusho*	reading

歌舞伎が大好きです。
kabuki ga daisuki desu
I love Kabuki theater.

セット
setto
set

3 **In conversation** (4 minutes)

カラオケに行きませんか？
karaoke ni ikimasenka

Do you want to go to a karaoke bar?

カラオケはきらいです。
karaoke wa kirai desu

I don't really like karaoke.

暇なときは何をしていますか？
hima na toki wa nani o shite imasuka

What do you do in your free time?

ビデオゲームが好きです。
bideo gehmu ga suki desu
I like video games.

俳優
haiyu
actor

舞台
butai
stage

4 Useful phrases (4 minutes)

Learn these phrases and then test yourself using the cover flap.

What do you do in your free time? (formal)	暇なときは何をしていますか？ *hima na toki wa nani o shite imasuka*
What do you do in your free time? (informal)	暇なとき何してる？ *hima na toki nani shiteru*
My hobby is reading.	趣味は読書です。 *shumi wa dokusho desu*
I prefer the movies.	私は映画の方が好きです。 *watashi wa eiga no hohga sukidesu*
I hate opera.	私はオペラは大嫌いです。 *watashi wa opera wa daikirai desu*

5 Say it (2 minutes)

I like music.

I prefer art.

My hobby is opera.

I hate theme parks.

ショッピングが好きです。
shoppingu ga suki desu

I like shopping.

私はショッピングは大嫌いです。
watashi wa shoppingu wa daikirai desu

I hate shopping.

良いですよ。一人で行きます。
ihdesuyo. hitori de ikimasu

No problem. I'll go on my own.

SUPOHTSU TO SHUMI
Sport and hobbies

Traditional Japanese sports include wrestling, martial arts, and fishing. These are still popular, but soccer, baseball, and golf have also established themselves. Arts and crafts include flower arranging, silk-screen painting, and calligraphy. Participating in tea ceremonies is also a popular hobby.

1 **Warm up** (1 minute)

What's the Japanese for "fish"? (pp.104-105)

Say "I like the theater" and "I prefer traveling." (pp.118-119)

Say "I don't really like ...." (pp.118-119)

2 **Words to remember** (5 minutes)

Memorize these words and then test yourself.

サッカー	*sakkah*	soccer
野球	*yakyu*	baseball
テニス	*tenisu*	tennis
水泳	*suiei*	swimming
登山	*tozan*	mountain climbing
魚釣り	*sakana tsuri*	fishing
絵を描くこと	*e o kaku koto*	painting
習字	*syu-ji*	calligraphy

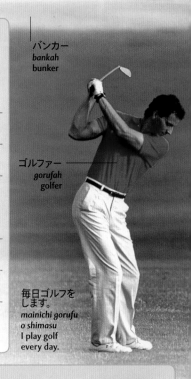

バンカー
bankah
bunker

ゴルファー
gorufah
golfer

毎日ゴルフをします。
mainichi gorufu o shimasu
I play golf every day.

3 **Useful phrases** (2 minutes)

Familiarize yourself with these phrases.

野球をします。 *yakyu o shimasu*	I play baseball.
彼はテニスをします。 *kare wa tenisu o shimasu*	He plays tennis.
彼女は絵を描くことが好きです。 *kanojyo wa e o kaku koto ga suki desu*	She likes painting.

4 Phrases to remember (4 minutes)

バイオリンを弾きます。
baiorin o hikimasu
I play the violin.

_____ フラッグ
furaggu
flag

_____ ゴルフコース
gorufu kohsu
golf course

Learn the phrases below and then test yourself.
Notice that *I play* is *shimasu* for sports but
hikimasu for musical instruments.

What do you like doing? (formal)	何をするのがお好きですか? *nani o surunoga osuki desuka*
What do you like doing? (informal)	何をするのが好き? *nani o surunoga suki*
I like playing golf.	ゴルフをするのが好きです。 *gorufu o surunoga suki desu*
I like playing baseball.	野球をするのが好きです。 *yakyu o surunoga suki desu*
I play tennis.	テニスをします。 *tenisu o shimasu*
I like going fishing.	私は魚釣りが好きです。 *watashi wa sakana tsuri ga suki desu*
I go mountain climbing.	登山に行きます。 *tozan ni ikimasu*

5 Put into practice (3 minutes)

Learn these phrases. Then cover up the text on the right and complete
the dialogue in Japanese. Check your answers.

何をするのがお好き
ですか?
nani o surunoga osuki desuka
What do you like doing?

Say: Playing soccer.

サッカーをするのが
好きです。
*sakkah o surunoga
suki desu*

野球もなさいますか?
yakyu mo nasai masuka
Do you play baseball
as well?

Say: No, I play golf.

いいえ、ゴルフをします。
ihe, gorufu o shimasu

よくプレーなさいますか?
yoku pureh nasai masuka
Do you play often?

Say: Every week.

毎週です。
maishu desu

SHAKOHTEKI NA BAMEN DE
Socializing

Say "(your) husband" and "(your) wife." (pp.12-13)

How do you say "lunch" and "dinner" in Japanese? (pp.20-21)

Say "Sorry, I'm busy that day." (pp.32-33)

As a business guest, it's more common to be invited to a restaurant than to someone's home. This is partly practical—people often have long commutes. But if you're staying for longer, you may be invited for a meal or a party.

2 **Useful phrases** (3 minutes)

Learn these phrases and then test yourself.

ディナーにいらっしゃいませんか? *dinah ni irasshai masenka*	Would you like to come for dinner?
水曜日はいかがですか? *suiyoh bi wa ikaga desuka*	What about Wednesday?
また今度誘ってください。 *mata kondo sasotte kudasai*	Perhaps another time.

Cultural tip When visiting a Japanese home, remember that it's customary to remove your outdoor shoes at the door. Take a gift for the host or hostess. Flowers, a bottle of wine, or a present from your home country will be very appreciated.

3 **In conversation** (6 minutes)

火曜日のディナーにいらっしゃいませんか?
kayoh bi no dinah ni irasshai masenka?

Would you like to come for dinner on Tuesday?

すみません。火曜日は忙しいです。
sumimasen. kayoh bi wa isogashih desu

Sorry. I'm busy on Tuesday.

木曜日はいかがですか?
mokuyoh bi wa ikaga desuka

What about Thursday?

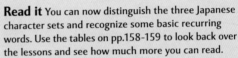

4 Words to remember (3 minutes)

Familiarize yourself with these words and test yourself using the flap.

party	パーティー	*pahtih*
invitation	招待	*shohtai*
gift	お土産	*omiyage*

招待者
shohtai sha
hostess

お客
okyaku
guest

Read it You can now distinguish the three Japanese character sets and recognize some basic recurring words. Use the tables on pp.158–159 to look back over the lessons and see how much more you can read.

5 Put into practice (2 minutes)

Join in this conversation.

土曜日にパーティーを開く
のですが、お暇ですか？
*doyoh bi ni pahtih o hiraku
no desuga, ohima desuka*

We are having a party on Saturday. Are you free?

Say: Yes, how nice!

はい、素敵ですね！
hai, suteki desune

ああよかった！
ah yokatta

That's great!

Say: At what time should we arrive?

何時に伺い
ましょうか？
nanji ni ukagai mashohka

ご招待ありがとう
ございます。
goshohtai arigatoh gozaimasu
Thank you for inviting us.

はい、素敵ですね！
hai, suteki desune

Yes, how nice!

ご主人もご一緒に。
goshujin mo goissho ni

Please bring your husband.

何時に伺いましょうか？
nanji ni ukagai mashohka

At what time should we arrive?

FUKUSHU TO KURIKAESHI

Review and repeat

1 Animals

❶ 猫
neko

❷ 鳥
tori

❸ 馬
uma

❹ 魚
sakana

❺ 犬
inu

1 Animals (3 minutes)

Name the numbered animals in Japanese.

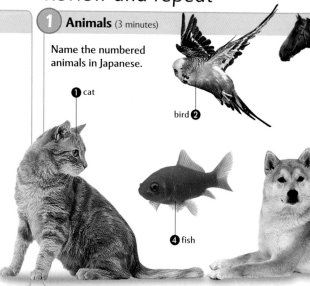

❶ cat

bird ❷

❹ fish

2 I like ...

❶ 野球をするのが好きです。
yakyu o surunoga suki desu

❷ ゴルフをするのが好きです。
gorufu o surunoga suki desu

❸ 私は絵を描くことが好きです。
watashi wa e o kaku koto ga suki desu

2 I like ... (4 minutes)

Say the following in Japanese.

❶ I like playing baseball.

❷ I like playing golf.

❸ I like painting.

❸ horse

❺ dog

3 Leisure (4 minutes)

What do these Japanese sentences mean?

❶ *karaoke wa daikirai desu*
❷ *bideo gehmu ga suki desu*
❸ *shumi wa dokusho desu*
❹ *watashi wa gekijyoh no hohga sukidesu*
❺ *baiorin o hikimasu*

3 Leisure

❶ *I hate karaoke.*
❷ *I like video games.*
❸ *My hobby is reading.*
❹ *I prefer the theater.*
❺ *I play the violin.*

4 An invitation (4 minutes)

You are invited for dinner. Join in the conversation, replying in Japanese following the English prompts.

doyoh bi no dinah ni irasshai masenka
❶ Sorry, I'm busy on Saturday.
mokuyoh bi wa ikaga desuka
❷ Yes, how nice!
goshujin mo goissho ni
❸ At what time should we arrive?
ichi ji han dewa
❹ Thank you very much.

4 An invitation

❶ すみません。
土曜日は忙しいです。
sumimasen. doyoh bi wa isogashih desu

❷ はい、素敵
ですね！
hai, suteki desune

❸ 何時に伺いましょうか？
nanji ni ukagai mashohka

❹ ありがとうございます。
arigatoh gozaimasu

Reinforce and progress

Regular practice is the key to maintaining and advancing your language skills. In this section, you will find a variety of suggestions for reinforcing and extending your knowledge of Japanese. Many involve returning to exercises in the book and using the dictionary to extend their scope. Go back through the lessons in a different order, mix and match activities to make up your own 15-minute daily program, or focus on topics that are of particular relevance to your current needs.

1 Warm up (1 minute)

Ask "How much is that?" (pp.18-19)

What are "breakfast," "lunch," and "dinner"? (pp.20-21)

What are "three," "four," "five," and "six"? (pp.10-11)

Stay warmed up
Revisit the Warm Up boxes to remind yourself of key words and phrases. Make sure you work your way through all of them on a regular basis.

2 I'd like ... (3 minutes)

Say "I'd like" the following:

4 tea   cake **1**

sugar **2**

coffee **3**

Review and repeat again
Work through a Review and Repeat lesson as a way of reinforcing words and phrases presented in the book. Return to the main lesson for any topic on which you are no longer confident.

3 In conversation: taxi (2 minutes)

Carry on conversing
Reread the In Conversation panels. Say both parts of the conversation, paying attention to the pronunciation. Where possible, try incorporating new words from the dictionary.

秋葉原までお願いします。
Akihabara ma-de onegai shimasu

To Akihabara, please.

わかりました。
wakarimashita

Very well.

ここで降ろしてください。
kokode oroshite kudasai

Can you drop me here, please?

4 Useful phrases (3 minutes)

Learn these phrases and then test yourself using the cover flap.

What time do you open?	何時に開きますか？ *nanji ni akimasuka*
What time does the store close?	店は何時に閉まりますか？ *mise wa nanji ni shimari masuka*
Is wheelchair access possible?	車いすは使えますか？ *kurumaisu wa tsukae masuka*

Practice phrases
Return to the Useful Phrases and Put into Practice exercises. Test yourself using the cover flap. When you are confident, devise your own versions of the phrases using new words from the dictionary.

Match, repeat, and extend

Remind yourself of words related to specific topics by returning to the Match and Repeat and Words to Remember exercises. Test yourself using the cover flap. Discover new words in that subject area by referring to the dictionary and menu guide.

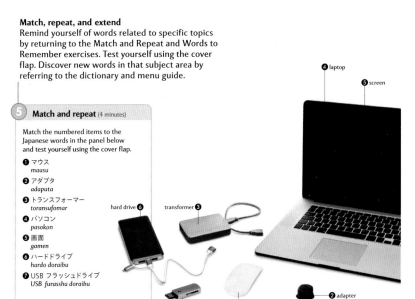

4 laptop

5 screen

hard drive **6**   transformer **3**

7 USB flash drive   **1** mouse

2 adapter

5 Match and repeat (4 minutes)

Match the numbered items to the Japanese words in the panel below and test yourself using the cover flap.

1 マウス
mausu

2 アダプタ
adaputa

3 トランスフォーマー
toransufomar

4 パソコン
pasokon

5 画面
gamen

6 ハードドライブ
hardo doraibu

7 USB フラッシュドライブ
USB furasshu doraibu

Say it again
The Say it exercises are a useful instant reminder for each lesson. Practice these using your own vocabulary variations from the dictionary or elsewhere in the lesson.

6 Say it (2 minutes)

What kind of flower is this?

I like the waterfall.

Is there a pond?

Using other resources

In addition to working with this book, try the following language extension ideas:

Visit Japan, if you can, and try out your new skills with native speakers. Otherwise, find out if there is a Japanese community near you. There may be stores, cafés, restaurants, and clubs. Try to visit some of these and use your Japanese to order food and drink and strike up conversations. Most native speakers will be happy to speak Japanese to you.

Join a language class or club. There are usually evening and day classes available at a variety of different levels. Or you could start a club yourself if you have friends who are also interested in keeping up their Japanese.

Practice your new knowledge of the Japanese scripts and characters (see pp.158-159). Look at the back of food packages and other products. You will often find a Japanese list of ingredients or components. See if you can spot some familiar words in the Japanese list and then compare them to the English equivalents.

Look at the titles and advertisements of Japanese magazines and manga comics. The pictures will help you to decipher the script. Look for familiar words and characters, even if you can't make out the whole text.

Use the internet to find websites for learning languages, some of which offer free online help.

MENU GUIDE

This guide lists the most common terms you may encounter on Japanese menus. Dishes are divided into categories, and the Japanese script is displayed clearly to help you identify items on a menu.

Appetizers and soups

hamu	ハム	ham
ohdoburu	オードブル	hors d'oeuvres
otsumami	おつまみ	Japanese appetizer
tsukidashi	つきだし	Japanese appetizer
ise-ebi	伊勢えび	lobster
meron	メロン	melon
minestorohne	ミネストローネ	minestrone
kuruma-ebi	車えび	shrimp
smohku sahmon	スモークサーモン	smoked salmon
misoshiru	みそ汁	soup made with fermented bean paste
tomato supu	トマトスープ	tomato soup

Egg dishes

behkon-eggu	ベーコンエッグ	bacon and eggs
tamago	卵	egg
medama-yaki	目玉焼き	fried eggs
hamu-eggu	ハムエッグ	ham and eggs
tamago-yaki	卵焼き	Japanese omelet
omuretsu	オムレツ	omelet
omuraisu	オムライス	rolled omelet filled with rice

chawan-mushi	茶碗蒸し	savory "custard" with egg and fish
tamago-dohfu	卵豆腐	steamed egg and tofu

Fish and sushi

awabi	あわび	abalone
suzuki	すずき／鱸	sea bass
fugu	フグ／河豚	blowfish
katsuo	かつお／鰹	bonito, tunny
unajyu	うな重	broiled eel on rice
koi	コイ／鯉	carp
nami	並	cheaper selection of fish
hamaguri	はまぐり／蛤	clam
tara	タラ／鱈	cod
tarako	タラコ	cod roe
anago	あなご	conger eel
kani	かに／蟹	crab
unagi	うなぎ／鰻	eel
joh	上	expensive selection
unadon	うな丼	grilled eel on rice
nishin	にしん／鰊	herring
kazunoko	かずのこ	herring roe
aji	あじ／鯵	horse mackerel
saba	さば／鯖	mackerel
gomoku-zushi	五目寿司	mixed sushi
chirashi-zushi	ちらし寿司	mixed sushi on rice

tako	たこ／蛸	octopus
oshi-zushi	押し寿司	Osaka-style sushi cut into squares
kaki	カキ／牡蠣	oyster
sashimi	刺身	raw fish
sushi	寿司／すし	raw fish on riceballs
nigiri-zushi	にぎり寿司	raw fish on riceballs
sake	さけ／鮭	salmon
ikura	イクラ	salmon roe
iwashi	いわし／鰯	sardines
hotategai	ホタテ貝	scallop
tai	タイ／鯛	sea bream
kappa-maki	カッパ巻き	seasoned rice and cucumber wrapped in seaweed
inari-zushi	いなり寿司	seasoned rice wrapped in fried tofu
uni	うに	sea urchin
ebi	えび／海老	shrimp
nori-maki	のり巻き	sliced roll of rice, vegetables, and fish powder, wrapped in seaweed
ika	イカ	squid
ayu	あゆ／鮎	sweet smelt
masu	マス／鱒	trout
maguro	まぐろ／鮪	tuna
kujira	くじら／鯨	whale
buri	ブリ／鰤	yellowtail

Meat and poultry

bahbekyu	バーベキュー	barbecue
gyu-niku	牛肉	beef
bihfu	ビーフ	beef
teppan-yaki	鉄板焼き	beef and vegetables grilled at the table
gyu-shohgayaki	牛しょうが焼き	beef cooked in soy sauce with ginger
bihfu-sutehki	ビーフステーキ	beef steak
niwatori	鶏	chicken
abaraniku	あばら肉	chops/ribs
korokke	コロッケ	croquettes
tonkatsu	とんかつ	deep-fried pork cutlets
katsudon	カツ丼	deep-fried pork cutlet on rice
kamo	鴨	duck
hireniku	ひれ肉	fillet
yakiniku	焼肉	fried pork marinated in soy sauce
kushiyaki	串焼き	grilled meat or vegetables on skewers
hanbahgah	ハンバーガー	hamburger
rebah	レバー	liver
niku	肉	meat
nikudango	肉団子	meat-filled dumplings
honetsuki	骨付き	on the bone
butaniku	豚肉	pork

buta-shohgayaki	豚しょうが焼き	pork cooked in soy sauce with ginger
uzura	うずら	quail
kareh-raisu	カレーライス	rice with curry-flavored stew
rohsuto-bihfu	ローストビーフ	roast beef
rohsuto-chikin	ローストチキン	roast chicken
rohsuto-pohku	ローストポーク	roast pork
sohsehji	ソーセージ	sausage
sahroin	サーロイン	sirloin
yakitori	焼き鳥	skewered chicken cooked over a grill
shabu-shabu	しゃぶしゃぶ	sliced beef with vegetables boiled in a pot at the table
sukiyaki	すき焼き	sliced beef with vegetables cooked at the table
spearibu	スペアリブ	spare ribs
suzume	すずめ	sparrow
stehki	ステーキ	steak

Rice dishes

...domburi	…丼	bowl of rice with something on top
unagidon	うなぎ丼	*domburi* with grilled eel
oyakodon	親子丼	*domburi* with chicken and egg
tendon	天丼	*domburi* with deep-fried seafood

tamagodon	卵丼	*domburi* cooked in egg with onions
chyukadon	中華丼	*domburi* with pork and vegetables
nikudon	肉丼	*domburi* with sliced beef
katsudon	カツ丼	*domburi* with deep-fried breaded pork cutlet
chah-han	チャーハン	fried rice
gohan/raisu	ご飯／ライス	rice
kamameshi	釜飯	rice steamed in fish stock with pieces of meat, fish, and vegetables
chikin raisu	チキンライス	rice with chicken
onigiri	おにぎり	rice balls wrapped in seaweed

Noodle dishes

rahmen	ラーメン	Chinese noodles
chahshumen	チャーシューメン	Chinese noodles in pork stock
chanpon	ちゃんぽん	Chinese noodles in salted stock with meat and vegetables
kanton-men	広東麺	Chinese noodles in salted pork-flavored soup with vegetables
soba	そば	long, brownish buckwheat noodles
udon	うどん	long, thick, white wheatflour noodles

sohmen	そうめん	long, thin, white wheatflour noodles (usually served cold in the summer)
wantan-men	ワンタンメン	noodle squares (wonton) containing ground pork and leeks, served in soup
tempura soba	天ぷらそば	noodles in fish stock with deep-fried shrimp
tsukimi soba	月見そば	noodles in fish stock with raw egg on top
niku udon	肉うどん	noodles in fish stock with pork or beef
kake soba	かけそば	simple dish of noodles in fish broth
kitsune udon	きつねうどん	noodles in fish broth with fried bean curd
chikara udon	力うどん	noodles in fish broth with rice cake (mochi)
moyashi soba	もやしそば	noodles in pork broth with bean sprouts
mori soba	盛りそば	noodles served cold, with sweetened soy sauce dip
miso rahmen	味噌ラーメン	noodles and pork in bean paste broth
gomoku soba	五目そば	soba noodles in broth with pieces of vegetables and meat

Vegetables, seasonings, and salads

aspara	アスパラ	asparagus
takenoko	竹の子	bamboo shoots
tohfu	豆腐	bean curd, tofu
mame	豆	beans
ohitashi	おひたし	boiled spinach with seasoning
kyabetsu	キャベツ	cabbage
ninjin	にんじん	carrot
kyu-ri	キュウリ	cucumber
nasu	なす	eggplant
miso	味噌	fermented soybean paste
nattoh	納豆	fermented soybeans
abura-age	油揚げ	fried bean curd
shohga	しょうが	ginger
pihman	ピーマン	green pepper
matsutake	松茸	Japanese mushrooms
nori	海苔	dried seaweed
retasu	レタス	lettuce
mayonehzu	マヨネーズ	mayonnaise
masshurumu	マッシュルーム	mushrooms
kinoko	きのこ	mushrooms (general term)
karashi	からし	mustard
abura	油	oil
tamanegi	玉ねぎ	onion
poteto/jyagaimo	ポテト／ジャガイモ	potatoes
poteto sarada	ポテトサラダ	potato salad

sarada	サラダ	salad
shio	塩	salt
shiokarai	塩辛い	salty
shohyu	醤油	soy sauce
daizu	大豆	soybeans
hohrensoh	ほうれん草	spinach
satoh	砂糖	sugar
amai	甘い	sweet
kohn	コーン	sweetcorn
tomato	トマト	tomato
yasai	野菜	vegetables
su	酢	vinegar
takuan	タクアン	yellow radish pickles

Japanese fixed menus

tehshoku	定食	fixed menu with rice, soup, pickles, and main dish
higawari	日替わり	*tehshoku* of the day
tempura	天ぷら	*tehshoku* with deep-fried shrimp, seafood, or vegetables as the main dish
yakiniku	焼肉	*tehshoku* with grilled meat as the main dish
tonkatsu	とんかつ	*tehshoku* with battered and deep-fried pork cutlet as the main dish

sashimi	刺身	*tehshoku* with raw fish as the main dish
ohiru no	お昼の	lunchtime *tehshoku*
bentoh	弁当	boxed lunch (sold at train stations, convenience stores, etc.)

Fruit and nuts

banana	バナナ	banana
cherih/sakurambo	チェリー／さくらんぼ	cherries
kuri	栗	chestnut
kokonattsu	ココナッツ	coconut
furu-tsu/kudamono	フルーツ／果物	fruit
gurehpu-furu-tsu	グレープフルーツ	grapefruit
remon	レモン	lemon
meron	メロン	melon
orenji	オレンジ	orange
pihchi/momo	ピーチ／桃	peach
kaki	柿	persimmon
painappuru	パイナップル	pineapple
kiichigo	ラズベリー／木苺	raspberry
sutoroberih/ichigo	ストロベリー／イチゴ	strawberries
mikan	みかん	tangerine
kurumi	クルミ	walnuts
suika	スイカ	watermelon

Desserts

appuru pai	アップルパイ	apple pie
kehki	ケーキ	cake
chihzu-kehki	チーズケーキ	cheesecake
chokorehto	チョコレート	chocolate
shu-kurihmu	シュークリーム	cream puff
kurehpu	クレープ	crêpe
uji-gohri	宇治氷	crushed ice with green tea syrup
kohri meron	氷メロン	crushed ice with melon syrup
dezahto	デザート	dessert
dohnatsu	ドーナツ	donut
mitsumame	みつ豆	gelatin cubes and sweet beans with pieces of fruit
aisukurihmu	アイスクリーム	ice cream
zerih	ゼリー	jelly
yohkan	ようかん	jelly with soft, sweet bean paste filling
mochi	もち	rice cakes (soft and glutinous when ready to eat)
senbeh	せんべい	rice crackers
manjyu	まんじゅう	rice-flour buns with bean paste
shohto kehki	ショートケーキ	"shortcake" (similar to sponge cake)
shahbetto	シャーベット	sorbet
sufure	スフレ	soufflé
kasutera	カステラ	sponge cake

sutoroberih aisukurihmu	ストロベリー アイスクリーム	strawberry ice cream
oshiruko	おしるこ	sweet bean soup with rice cake
purin	プリン	vanilla egg custard with brown sugar
banira aisukurihmu	バニラ アイスクリーム	vanilla ice cream
kurihmu anmitsu	クリームあんみつ	vanilla ice cream with seaweed jelly, sweet beans, and fruit
yohguruto	ヨーグルト	yogurt

Western snacks

pan	パン	bread
batah	バター	butter
chihzu-rohru	チーズロール	cheese roll
furaido chikin	フライドチキン	fried chicken
hamusando	ハムサンド	ham sandwich
jamu	ジャム	jam
ranchi	ランチ	lunch
mahmarehdo	マーマレード	marmalade
piza	ピザ	pizza
sando icchi	サンドイッチ	sandwich
spagetti	スパゲッティ	spaghetti
tohsto	トースト	toast

Drinks

nomimono	飲み物	beverages
bihru	ビール	beer
kohcha	紅茶	black tea ("red tea")
kokoah	ココア	cocoa, hot chocolate
koh-hi	コーヒー	coffee
kohra	コーラ	cola
shohchyu	焼酎	Japanese vodka
nama bihru	生ビール	draft beer
sohda sui	ソーダ水	green, sweet, carbonated drink
ocha/ryokucha	お茶／緑茶	Japanese tea
remon tih	レモンティー	lemon tea
miruk/gyunyu	ミルク／牛乳	milk
miruku shehku	ミルクシェイク	milkshake
mineraru wohtah	ミネラル ウォーター	mineral water
orenji sukasshu	オレンジ スカッシュ	orange cordial
orenji jyu-su	オレンジジュース	orange juice
pain jyu-su	パインジュース	pineapple juice
sake/nihon-shu	酒／日本酒	rice wine
saidah	サイダー	soda
miruku tih	ミルクティー	tea with milk
tomato jyu-su	トマトジュース	tomato juice
tonikku wohtah	トニック ウォーター	tonic water
uisukih	ウイスキー	whisky
onzarokku	オンザロック	(whisky) on the rocks
mizuwari	水割り	(whisky) with water

wain/budohshu	ワイン／ぶどう酒	wine
edamame	枝豆	soybeans in the pod served as snacks with drinks

Chinese meals

subuta	酢豚	a kind of sweet-and-sour pork
mahboh-dohfu	マーボー豆腐	bean curd in spicy meat sauce mixture
chu-ka ryohri	中華料理	Chinese food
harumaki	春巻き	deep-fried spring roll
gyohza	餃子	fried dumplings stuffed with minced pork
kurage no	くらげの	sliced parboiled jellyfish
shu-mai	シュウマイ	small steamed pork dumplings in thin Chinese phyllo pastry
niku-man	肉まん	steamed dumplings filled with seasoned minced pork

Festival food

yaki-imo	焼き芋	baked sweet potato
watagashi	綿菓子	cotton candy
ikayaki	イカ焼き	charcoal-grilled squid
takoyaki	たこ焼き	griddle-fried octopus (in batter)
oden	おでん	hodgepodge of fish and vegetables boiled in fish broth
amaguri	甘栗	roasted chestnuts
tohmorokoshi	とうもろこし	roasted corn on the cob
okonomiyaki	お好み焼き	Japanese-style savory pancakes
tako senbeh	たこせんべい	shrimp-flavored pink crackers

Cooking methods and styles

robatayaki	炉端焼き	charcoal-grilled fish and vegetables
okashi	お菓子	confectionery
kappoh	割烹	special order Japanese-style dishes
agemono	揚げ物	deep-fried foods
tempura	天ぷら	deep-fried seafood and vegetables in batter
nabemono	鍋物	food cooked in a pot at the table
sunomono	酢の物	foods with vinegar
yakimono	焼き物	grilled foods
kaiseki ryohri	懐石料理	Japanese haute cuisine
nihon shoku/washoku	日本食／和食	Japanese-style cuisine

men rui	麺類	noodle dishes
tsukemono	漬物	pickled foods
tori-ryohri	鳥料理	poultry dishes
kyohdo ryohri	郷土料理	regional specialities
gohan-mono	ご飯もの	rice dishes
nimono	煮物	simmered foods
shirumono	汁物	soups
mushimono	蒸し物	steamed foods
shohjin ryohri	精進料理	ascetic, monastic style of vegetarian cooking
sehyoh ryohri	西洋料理	Western-style cuisine

DICTIONARY
English to Japanese

The plural is normally the same as the singular in Japanese. In general, Japanese descriptive words, or adjectives, may change depending on how they are used. Some of these adjectives are followed by *(no)* or *(na)*. If a noun is used following such a word, then the **no** or **na** must be put after the adjective: ***kanojo wa kireh desu*** (*she is pretty*); ***kanojo wa kireh na jyoseh desu*** (*she is a pretty girl*).

A

about: about 16 *jyu-roku kurai*
accelerator *akuseru*
accident *jiko*
accommodations *heya*
accountant *kaikehshi*
ache *itami*
across from: across from the hotel *hoteru no hantai gawa*
actor *haiyu*
adapter (electrical) *adaputa*
address *jyu-sho*
adhesive tape *serotehpu*
admission charge *nyujoh ryoh*
after *ato*
afternoon *gogo*
aftershave lotion *afutah-shehbu-rohshon*
again *mata*
against *hantai*
agenda *kaigi jikoh*
air conditioning *eakon*
air freshener *ea-furesshnah*
air hostess *ea-hosutesu*
air mail *ea mehru*
airline *kohku-gaisha*
airplane *hikohki*
airport *ku-koh*
alcohol *arukohru*
all *zembu* **that's all, thanks** *arigatoh, sore de zenbu desu*
almost *hotondo*
alone *hitori de*
already *sudeni*
always *itsmo*
am: I am British *watashi wa igirisu jin desu*
ambulance *kyu-kyu-sha*
America *Amerika*
American (person) *amerika jin* (adj) *amerika no*
and (with nouns) *to* (with verbs) *soshite*
ankle *ashikubi*

anniversary *kinenbi*
another (different) *betsu (no)* (further) *moh hitotsu (no)*
answering machine *rusuban denwa*
antifreeze *futohzai*
antique store *kottoh hin ten*
antiseptic *bohfuzai/ shohdokuzai*
apartment *apahto*
appetite *shokuyoku*
apple *ringo*
application form *mohshkomisho*
appointment *(go)yoyaku; apo*
apricot *anzu*
April *shi gatsu*
architecture (field of study) *kenchiku gaku*
are: you are very kind *anata wa totemo shinsetsu desu* **we are British** *watashi tachi wa igirisu jin desu* **they are Japanese** *karera wa nihonjin desu*
arm *ude*
arrivals *tohchaku*
art *ahto; bijutsu*
art gallery *bijutsukan*
artist *geijutsuka*
as: as soon as possible *dekiru dake hayaku*
ashtray *haizara*
Asia *Ajia*
asleep: he's asleep *kare wa nemutte imasu*
aspirin *aspirin*
asthmatic: I'm asthmatic *zensoku mochi desu*
at: at the post office *yu-bin kyoku de* **at night** *yoru* **at 3 o'clock** *san ji ni*
ATM *"ATM"*
attic *yane ura*
attractive *miryokuteki (na)*
August *hachi gatsu*
aunt *oba(san)*

Australia *Ohsutoraria*
Australian (person) *ohsutoraria jin* (adj) *ohsutoraria no*
automatic *jidoh*
away: is it far away? *tohi desuka* **go away!** *atchi e itte*
awful *hidoi*
ax *ono*
axle *shajiku*

B

baby *akachan*
baby wipes *bebih waipu*
back *ushiro* (upper back, body) *senaka* (lower back, body) *koshi*
backpack *ryukku sakku*
bacon *behkon* **bacon and eggs** *behkon-eggu*
bad *warui*
bakery *pan ya*
balcony *barukonih*
ball *bohru* (dance) *butohkai*
ball-point pen *bohru-pen*
banana *banana*
band (musicians) *bando*
bandage *hohtai*
bandage (for cut) *bansohkoh*
bank *ginkoh*
bar *bah* **bar of chocolate** *itachoko*
barbershop *riyoh in*
bargain *bahgen*
baseball *yakyu*
basement *chika*
basin (sink) *sen-mendai*
basket *kago*
bath *ofuro/basu* **to take a bath** *ofuro ni hairu*
bathroom *basu (ru-mu); ofuroba*
battery *batteri; denchi*
beach *hamabe/kaigan*

beans *mame*
beard *hige*
beautiful *utsukushih*
beauty products *keshoh hin*
beauty salon *biyoh in*
because *(da)kara*
 because it is too big
 ohki-suguru kara
bed *beddo*
bed and breakfast
 chohshoku to yu-shoku tsuki
bed linen *shihtsu to*
 makurakabah
bedroom *shinshitsu/*
 beddo ru-mu
bedspread *beddo supureddo*
beef *gyu-niku*
beer *bihru*
before *mae ni*
beginner *shoshinsha*
behind *ushiro*
beige *behju*
bell *beru*
below *shita*
belt *beruto*
beside *soba*
best *ichiban ih*
better *motto ih*
between *aida ni*
bicycle *jitensha*
big *ohkih*
bikini *bikini*
bill *okanjoh*
bills (money) *shiheh*
bird *tori*
birthday *taniyoh bi*
 happy birthday!
 otaniyoh bi omedetoh
 birthday present
 taniyoh bi no purezento
biscuit *bisketto*
bite (verb) *kamu* (by insect)
 mushi sasare
bitter (adj) *nigai*
black *kuro*
blanket *mohfu*
blind (cannot see) *mohmoku*
 (no) (on window) *buraindo*
blister *mizu-bukure*
blood *ketsueki/chi*
 blood test *ketsueki kensa*
blouse *burausu*
blue *ao*
boat *fune*
body *karada*
boil (verb: water) *wakasu*
 (noun: on body) *hare-mono*
boiled *yudeta*
bolt (on door) *boruto*
bone *hone*
book (noun) *hon*

(verb) *yoyaku suru*
 bookstore *hon ya*
boot *bu-tsu*
border *kokkyoh*
boring *tsumaranai*
born: I was born in ... (place)
 watashi wa... de umare-
 mashita (year) *watashi wa...*
 nen ni umare-mashita
both *ryohhoh*
 both of them *futari tomo*
 both of us *watashi tachi*
 futari
 both ... and ... *...to...*
bottle *bin*
bottle opener *sennuki*
bottom (of box, sea) *soko*
bowl *bohru*
box *hako*
box office *kippu uriba*
boy *otoko no ko*
boyfriend *bohi-furendo*
bra *burajah*
bracelet *udewa/*
 buresuretto
brake (noun) *burehki*
 (verb) *burehki o kakeru*
branch (office) *shiten*
brandy *burandeh*
bread *pan*
breakdown (car) *koshoh*
 (nervous) *shinkei-suijaku*
breakfast *chohshoku*
breathe *iki o suru*
 I can't breathe
 iki ga dekimasen
bridge *hashi*
briefcase *kaban*
British/English (nationality/
 things) *igirisu no*
 the British *igirisu jin*
brochure *panfuretto*
broken *kowareta*
 ... is broken *...ga*
 kowarete imasu
 broken leg *kossetsu*
 shita ashi
brooch *burohchi*
brother (older) *onihsan*
 (younger) *otohto*
brown *cha-iro* (no)
bruise *dabokushoh/*
 uchimi
brush (noun) *burashi*
bucket *baketsu*
Buddha *Hotoke*
Buddhism *Bukkyoh*
Buddhist (noun) *Bukkyohto*
 (adj) *Bukkyoh no*
budget (noun) *yosan*
builder *kenchiku ka*

building *tatemono/biru*
bumper *banpah*
burglar *doroboh/yatoh*
burn (verb) *moyasu*
 (noun) *yakedo*
bus *basu*
business *shigoto; bijinesu*
business card *meishi*
businessman *kaisha in*
bus station *basu teh*
busy (person) *isogashih*
 (crowded) *konzatsu shita*
but *demo*
butcher *niku ya*
butter *batah*
button *botan*
buy *kau*
by: by the window *mado no*
 soba **by Friday** *kinyoh bi*
 ma-de ni **by myself** *jibun de*

C

cabbage *kyabetsu*
cabinet (kitchen) *todana*
cable car *kehburu kah*
cable TV *kehbru terebi*
café *kafe/kissaten*
cake *kehki*
 cake shop *kehki ya*
calculator *kehsanki*
call: what's it called?
 nan to ihmasuka
calligraphy *shu-ji*
camera *kamera*
can *kanzume* **can I**
 have ...? *...o onegai shimasu*
can (tin) *kan*
can opener *kankiri*
Canada *Kanada*
Canadian (person) *kanada jin*
 (adj) *kanada no*
cancer *gan*
candle *rohsoku*
cap (bottle) *futa* (hat) *bohshi*
car *kuruma*
car seat (for a baby)
 bebih shihto
carbonated *tansan no*
carburetor *kyaburetah*
card (business) *meishi*
cardigan *kahdigan*
careful *chu-i-bukai*
 be careful! *ki o tsukete*
carpenter *daiku*
carpet *jyu-tan/kahpetto*
carriage (train) *kyakusha*
carrot *ninjin*
carry-cot *akachan yoh*
 kehtai beddo
case (suitcase) *su-tsu-kehsu*

cash (money) *genkin* (coins)
kohka/koin **to pay cash**
genkin de harau
cashier (bank, etc.)
madoguchi
cassette *kasetto*
cassette player
kasetto purehyah
castle *shiro*
cat *neko*
cave *hora-ana/dohkutsu*
CD drive *CD doraibu*
ceiling *ten-jyoh*
cellphone *kehtai (denwa)*
cemetery *bochi*
center *sentah*
certificate *shohmeisho*
chair *isu*
  swivel chair *kaiten isu*
chambermaid *meido*
change (noun: money) *otsuri*
  (verb: general) *kaeru*
  (verb: transport) *norikaeru*
character (written) *ji*
charger (electrical) *chahjyah*
cheap *yasui*
check (payment) *kogitte*
check-in *chekku in*
checkbook *kogitte choh*
checkout (hotel) *chekkuauto*
  (supermarket) *reji*
cheers! *kanpai*
cheese *chihzu*
cherry *sakurambo/cherih*
chess *chesu*
chest *mune*
chewing gum *chu-in-gamu*
chicken *niwatori*
child *kodomo*
children *kodomotachi*
  children's ward
  shohni byohtoh
china *tohki*
China *Chyugoku*
Chinese (person) *chyugoku
jin* (adj) *chyugoku no*
chips *chippu*
chocolate *chokorehto*
  box of chocolates
  hakozume no chokorehto
chop (noun: food) *choppu*
  (to cut) *kizamu*
chopstick rest *ohashi-oki*
chopsticks *ohashi*
Christian name *namae*
church *kyohkai*
cigar *hamaki*
cigarette *tabako*
city *toshi/machi*
city center *chu shingai*
class: (train)

first class *ittoh sha*
  second class *nitoh sha*
classical music
  kurasshikku ongaku
clean (adj) *kireh (na)*
cleaner *seisoh gyohsha*
clear (obvious) *meihaku (na)*
  (water) *sumikitta*
  is that clear?
  wakari-masuka
clever *kashikoi*
client *kokyaku*
clock *tokei* (alarm)
  mezamashi-dokei
close (near) *chikai*
  (stuffy) *iki-gurushih*
  (verb) *shimeru*
  we close at six o'clock
  roku ji ni
clothes *fuku*
clothespin
  sentaku-basami
club *kurabu* (cards) *kurabu*
coach *choh-kyori basu*
  (of train) *kyakusha*
coach station *basu
  hacchaku jyo*
coat *kohto*
coathanger *hangah*
cockroach *gokiburi*
coffee *koh-hih*
coins *kohka/koin*
cold (illness) *kaze* (weather)
  samui (food, etc.) *tsumetai*
collar *eri*
collection (stamps, etc.)
  shu-shu
color *iro*
color film *karah firumu*
comb (noun) *kushi* (verb) *toku*
come *kuru* **come to my
  party** *pahtih ni kitene*
  come here! *koko ni kinasai*
  I come from ... *...jin desu*
compartment *shikiri
  kyakushitsu*
complicated *fukuzatsu (na)*
computer *konpyu-tah*
  computer repair store
  konpyu-tah shu-ri ten
concert *ongakukai/konsahto*
conditioner (hair) *rinsu/
  kondishonah*
conductor (orchestra)
  shikisha
conference (meeting)
  konferensu (academic) *gakkai*
congratulations! *omedetoh*
constipation *bempi*
consul *ryohji*
consulate *ryohjikan*

contact lenses
  kontakuto renzu
contraceptive *hinin-yaku*
  (pills) *hiningu/kondohmu*
contract (noun) *kehyaku sho*
cook (person) *kokku*
  (verb) *ryohri suru*
cooking utensils
  ryohri-dohgu
cool *suzushih*
cork *koruku*
corkscrew *sen-nuki*
corner *kado*
corridor *rohka*
cosmetics *keshohhin*
cost (verb) *kakaru*
  what does it cost?
  ikura kakari-masuka
cotton *kotton*
cotton wool *dasshimen*
couch *sofa*
cough (noun) *seki*
cough drops *nodo gusuri/
  nodo ame*
counter (kitchen) *chohridai*
country (state) *kuni*
  (not town) *inaka*
cousin *itoko*
cow *ushi*
crab *kani*
cramp *keiren*
crayfish *zarigani*
cream (for face, food)
  kurihmu
credit card *kurejitto kahdo*
crime *hanzai*
crosswalk *ohdan hodoh*
crowded *konzatsu shita*
cruise *kohkai/kuru-zu*
crutches *matsubazue*
cry (weep) *naku*
  (shout) *sakebu*
cucumber *kyuri*
cuff links *kafusu botan*
cup *kappu*
cupboard *todana*
curlers *kahrah*
curry *kareh*
curtains *kahten*
customs *zeikan*
cut (noun) *kirikizu* (verb) *kiru*

D

dad *otohsan*
daily planner *techoh*
dairy (products) *nyu seihin*
damp *shimetta*
dance *dansu*
dangerous *abunai*
dark *kurai*

daughter *musume san*
  my daughter *musume*
day *hizuke/hi/nichi*
dead *shinda*
deaf *mimi ga tohi*
dear (person) *shitashih*
December *jyu-ni gatsu*
deck chair *dekki che-ah*
deep *fukai*
deliberately *wazato*
delivery *haitatsu*
dentist *ha-isha*
dentures *ireba*
deodorant *deodoranto*
department
  (of company, etc.) *bu*
department store *depahto*
departures *shuppatsu*
designer *dezainah*
desk *tsukue/desuku*
develop (a film) *genzoh suru*
diabetic: I'm diabetic
  tohnyoh byoh desu
diamond (jewel) *daiyamondo*
  (cards) *daiya*
diapers *omutsu*
  disposable diapers
  kami omutsu
diarrhea *geri*
diary *nikki*
dictionary *jisho*
die *shinu*
diesel *dihzeru*
different *chigau/betsu (no)*
  I'd like a different one
  betsu no ga hoshih desu
difficult *muzukashih*
dining car *shokudohsha*
dining room *dainingu
  ru-mu; shokudoh*
dinner *yu-shoku/dinah*
directory (telephone)
  denwachoh
dirty *kitanai*
disabled *karada no fujiyu (na)*
dishwasher *shokki araiki*
dishwashing liquid *shokki
  yoh senzai*
distributor (in car) *haidenki*
dive *tobikomu*
diving board *tobikomi-dai*
divorced *rikonshita*
do *suru*
dock *hatoba*
doctor *isha*
document *shohsho;
  dokyumento*
dog *inu*
doll *nin-gyoh*
dollar *doru*
donut *dohnatsu*

door *doa*
double room (hotel)
  daburu ru-mu
  (ryokan) *hutari-beya*
down *shita*
drawer *hikidashi*
dress (noun) *doresu*
drink (verb) *nomu*
  (noun) *nomimono*
drinking water *nomimizu*
drive (verb) *untensuru*
driver *untenshu*
driver's license
  unten menkyosho
drops (for eyes) *megusuri*
dry *kawaita*
dry cleaner *dorai
  kurihningu ya*
during: during ... ...no aida ni*
duster *dasutah*
duty-free *menzei*

E

each (every) *sorezore*
  200 yen each
  sorezore ni-hyaku yen desu
ear *mimi*
earbuds *iyafon*
early *hayai*
earrings *iyaringu*
east *higashi*
East Asia *Kyokutoh*
easy *yasashih/kantan (na)*
egg *tamago*
eight *hachi*
eighteen *jyu-hachi*
eighty *hachi-jyu*
either: either of them
  dochira demo
  either ... or ... *...ka...*
elastic (noun) *gomuhimo*
elastic band *wagomu*
elbow *hiji*
electric *denki no*
electrician *denki gishi*
electricity *denki*
electronics *denshi-kohgaku*
electronics store *denkiya*
elevator *erebehtah*
eleven *jyu-ichi*
else: something else
  nanika hokano mono
  someone else
  dareka hokano hito
  anything else?
  nanika hoka ni
email (ih) *mehru*
  email address
  (ih) *mehru adoresu*
embarrassing *hazukashih*

embassy *taishikan*
embroidery *shishyu*
emerald *emerarudo*
emergency *hijoh*
  emergency room
  kyu-kyu byohtoh
emperor *tennoh*
empty *kara (no)*
end *owari*
engaged (couple) *konyaku
  shita* (telephone)
  hanashichu
engine (motor) *enjin*
engineering (field of study)
  kohgaku
England *Igirisu*
English (language) *eigo*
Englishman *igirisu jin*
Englishwoman *igirisu jin*
enlargement (of
  photography) *hikinobashi*
enough *jyu-bun*
entertainment *goraku*
entrance *nyu-jyoh guchi/
  iriguchi*
envelope *fu-toh*
epileptic: I'm epileptic
  tenkan mochi desu
escalator *esukarehtah*
especially *tokuni*
estimate (noun) *mitsumori*
Europe *Yohroppa*
evening *yu-gata/yoru*
  good evening *konbanwa*
every (morning, day, etc.)
  mai- (all) *subete no*
everyone *minna*
everything *minna/zenbu*
everywhere *doko demo*
executive (person) *jyu-yaku*
exhibition *tenji kai*
example *rei*
  for example *tatoeba*
excellent *saikoh/subarashih*
excess luggage
  chohka-nimotsu
exchange (verb) *kohkan suru*
  can I exchange this?
  kohkan dekimasuka
exchange rate *rehto*
excursion *ensoku/
  kankoh ryokoh*
excuse me! *shitsurei
  shimasu/sumimasen*
exit *deguchi*
expensive *takai*
explain *setsumei suru*
extension (telephone) *naisen*
  (lengthening) *kakuchoh*
eye *meh*
eyebrow *mayu*

F

face *kao*
faint (unclear) *usui/bonyari shita* (verb) *kizetsu suru*
  to feel faint *memai ga suru*
fair (entertainment) *yu-enchi*
  it's not fair *fukohhei desu*
fall (season) *aki*
false teeth *ireba/gishi*
family *kazoku*
fan (folding fan) *sensu* (electric) *senpu-ki* (enthusiast) *fan*
fan belt *fan beruto*
far *toh-i* is it far from here? *koko kara toh-i desuka*
fare *unchin; ryohkin*
farm *nohjoh*
farmer *nohfu*
fashion *fasshon*
fast *hayai*
fat (of person) *futotta* (on meat, etc.) *abura/shiboh*
father *otohsan*
  my father *chichi*
faucet *jyaguchi*
February *ni gatsu*
feel (touch) *sawaru*
  I feel hot *atsui desu*
  I feel like ... *...no yoh na ki ga shimasu*
felt-tip pen *feruto pen*
ferry *ferih*
fever *netsu*
fiancé *konyakusha/fianse*
field (agricultural) *nohara*
  what's your field? *gosenmon wa*
fifteen *jyu-go*
fifty *go-jyu*
fig *ichijiku*
figures (sales, etc.) *gohkeh gaku*
filling (tooth) *ha no jyu-ten* (sandwich) *nakami*
film (movies) *eiga* (camera) *firumu*
filter *firutah*
finger *yubi*
fire *hi* (blaze) *honoh*
fire extinguisher *shohkaki*
firework *hanabi*
first *saisho (no)*
first aid *ohkyu teate*
first floor *ikkai*
fish *sakana*
fishing *sakana tsuri*
  to go fishing *tsuri ni iku*

fishing rod *tsuri zao*
five *go*
flag *hata; furaggu*
flash (camera) *furasshu*
flat (level) *taira (na)*
flat tire *panku*
flavor *aji*
flea *nomi*
flight *hikoh(ki)*
  flight number ... *...bin*
  flight attendant *kyakushitsu jyohmu in*
flip-flops *zohri*
flippers *hire-ashi*
floor (of room) *yuka*
florist *hana ya*
flour *komugiko*
flower *hana*
flute *furu-to*
fly (verb) *tobu* (insect) *hae*
fog *kiri*
folk music *minzoku ongaku/fohku myu-jikku*
food *tabemono*
food poisoning *shoku chyudoku*
foot (on body) *ashi*
for: for ... *...no tame ni*
  for me *watashi no tame ni*
  what for? *nan no tame ni*
  for a week *isshu-kan*
foreigner *gaikoku jin*
forest *mori*
fork *fohku*
fortnight *ni-shu-kan*
forty *yon-jyu*
fountain *funsui*
fountain pen *mannen-hitsu*
four *shi/yon*
fourteen *jyu-yon/jyu-shi*
fourth *yombamme*
fracture *kossetsu*
free *jiyu (na)* (no cost) *muryoh*
freezer *reitohko*
french fries *poteto-furai*
Friday *kin-yoh bi*
fried *ageta*
friend *tomodachi*
friendly *shitashimi no aru/furendorih na*
front: in front of ... *...no mae ni*
frost *shimo*
frozen foods *reitoh shokuhin*
fruit *kudamono/furu-tsu*
fruit juice *furu-tsu jyu-su*
fry *ageru*
frying pan *furai pan*
full *ippai*
  I'm full *onaka ga*

ippai desu
full board *shokuji tsuki*
funny *omoshiroi* (odd) *okashih*
furnished: is it furnished? *kagu tsuki desuka*
furniture *kagu*

G

garage (parking) *shako* (gasoline) *gassorin sutando* (repairs) *shu-ri ya*
garbage (refuse) *gomi* (poor quality) *garakuta*
garbage can *gomibako*
garden *niwa*
garlic *ninniku*
gas station *gassorin sutando*
gasoline *gasorin*
gate (airport) *tohjyoh guchi/gehto*
gay (happy) *yohki (na)* (homosexual) *homosekusharu*
gear *giya*
gear lever *giya rebah*
geisha (girl) *geisha*
get *motte kuru*
  have you got ...? *...o omochi desuka*
  to get to the train *densha ni noru*
get back: we get back tomorrow *ashita kaerimasu*
  to get something back *kaeshite morau*
get in (to car, etc.) *noru* (arrive) *tsuku*
get out (of bus, etc.) *oriru*
get up (rise) *okiru*
gift *omiyage; okurimono*
gin *jin*
girl *onna no ko*
girlfriend *gahrufurendo*
give *ageru*
glad *ureshih*
  I'm glad *ureshih desu*
glass *gurasu* (for drinking) *gurasu*
glasses *megane*
glossy prints *kohtaku no aru purinto*
gloves *tebukuro*
glue *nori*
go *iku* where are you going? *doko iku no*
  I'm going to ... *...ni ikimasu*
goggles *suichu megane*
gold *kin*

golf *gorufu*
golfer *gorufah*
good *ih* good! *yokatta*
good morning
ohayo gozaimasu
good evening *konbanwa*
goodbye (informal) *sayonara*;
(formal) *sayohnara*
government *seifu*
granddaughter
mago-musume
grandfather *ojihsan*
my grandfather *sofu*
grandmother *obahsan*
my grandmother *sobo*
grandson *mago-musko*
grapes *budoh*
grass *kusa*
gray *hai-iro (no)*
Great Britain *Igirisu*
green *midori/gurihn*
grill *guriru*
grilled *yaita*
grocery store
shokuryoh hinten
ground floor *ikkai*
guarantee (noun) *hoshoh-sho*
(verb) *hoshoh suru*
guidebook *gaido bukka*
guided tour *gaido*
tsuki tsuah
guitar *gitah*
gun (rifle) *jyu/raifuru*
(pistol) *pisutoru*
gutter *amadoi*

H

hair *kami*
hair dryer *doraiyah*
hair spray *heya supureh*
haircut (for man) *sanpatsu*
(for woman) *katto*
half *hanbun*
half an hour *sanjippun*
ham *hamu*
hamburger *hanbahgah*
hammer *kanazuchi*
hand *te*
hand brake *hando burehki*
handbag *handobaggu*
handkerchief *hankachi*
handle (door) *handoru*
handsome *hansamu (na)*
hangover *futsuka-yoi*
happen: when did
it happen? *itsu*
okori mashitaka
happy *shiawase (na)*
harbor *minato*
hard *katai*

(difficult) *muzukashih*
hard lenses (contact)
hahdo renzu
hardware store *kanamono*
ya
harmony *chohwa/hahmonih*
hat *bohshi*
hate: I hate ... *watashi wa...*
ga daikirai desu
have *motsu*
I have ... *...wa/ga arimasu/*
imasu; ...o motte imasu
I don't have ...
...wa/ga arimasen/imasen;
...o motte imasen
can I have ...? *...o kudasai*
have you got ...?
...o omochi desuka
I have a headache
zutsu ga shimasu
hay fever *kafunshoh*
he *kare*
head *atama*
headache *zutsu*
headlights *heddo raito*
headquarters *honsha*
hear *kiku*
hearing aid *hochohki*
heart *shinzoh*
heart attack *shinzoh mahi*
heating *danboh*
heavy *omoi*
heel *kakato*
hello! *konnichiwa*
(on the telephone)
moshi moshi
help (noun) *enjo/tasuke*
(verb) *taskeru*
help! *taskete*
hepatitis *kan-en*
her: it's her *kanojo desu*
it's for her *kanojo no desu*
give it to her *kanojo ni*
agete kudasai
her book(s) *kanojo no hon*
it's hers *kanojo no*
(mono) desu
high *takai*
highway *kohsoku-dohro*
hill *oka*
him: it's him *kare desu*
it's for him *kare no desu*
give it to him *kare ni*
agete kudasai
hire *kariru*
his: his shoe(s) *kare no kutsu*
it's his *kare no (mono) desu*
history *rekishi*
hitchhike *hicchi-haiku*
HIV positive *eichi ai bui*
kansensya

hobby *shumi*
holiday (public) *kyu jitsu*
home *ie*
homeopathy *dohshu*
ryoh hoh
honest *shohjiki (na)*
honey *hachimitsu*
honeymoon *shinkon-ryokoh*
hood (car) *bonn-netto*
horn (car) *kurakushon*
horrible *osoroshih*
horse *uma*
hospital *byoh-in*
hot *atsui*
hot chocolate *kokoah*
hot water bottle *yutampo*
hotel *hoteru*
hour *jikan*
house *ie*
household products
katei yo-hin
housewife *sengyo-shufu*
how? *doh*
how much? *ikura desuka*
hundred *hyaku*
hungry: I'm hungry
onaka ga suite imasu
hurry: I'm in a hurry
isoide imasu
hurt: will it hurt?
itai desuka
husband *goshujin*
my husband *otto*

I

I *watashi*
ice *kohri*
ice cream *aisukurihmu*
ice pop *aiskyandeh*
if *moshi*
ignition *tenka sohchi*
ill *byohki*
immediately *suguni*
impossible *fukanoh*
in: in Japan *Nihon ni*
in Japanese *Nihongo de*
in my room *watashi no*
heya ni
India *Indo*
Indian (person) *indo jin*
(adj) *indo no*
indicator *winkah*
indigestion *shohka-furyoh*
infection *kansen*
information *johhoh*
information desk
madoguchi
inhaler (for asthma, etc.)
kyu-nyu-ki
injection *chu-sha*

injury *kega*
ink *inku*
inn (traditional Japanese) *ryokan*
insect *mushi*
insect repellent *mush-sasare yobohyaku*
insomnia *fuminshoh*
insurance *hoken*
interesting *omoshiroi*
internet *intahnetto*
internet café *netto kafeh*
interpret *tsu-yaku suru*
invitation *shohtai*
invoice (noun) *sehkyu-sho*
Ireland *Airurando*
Irish *Airurando no*
Irishman *airurando jin*
Irishwoman *airurando jin*
iron (metal) *tetsu*
  (for clothes) *airon*
is: he/she/it is ... *kare wa/kanojo wa/ sore wa... desu*
island *shima*
it *sore*
itch (noun) *kayumi*
  it itches *kayui desu*

J

jacket *jyaketto*
jacuzzi *jagujih*
jam *jamu*
January *ichi gatsu*
Japan *Nihon*
Japanese (person) *nihonjin*
  (adj) *nihon no*
  (language) *nihongo*
Japanese-style *wafu*
jazz *jazu*
jealous *shitto-bukai*
jeans *jihnzu*
jellyfish *kurage*
jewelry store *hohseki shoh*
job *shigoto*
jog (verb) *jogingu suru*
  to go for a jog *jogingu ni iku*
joke *johdan*
journey *ryokoh/tabi*
July *shichi gatsu*
jumper *jampah/sehtah*
June *roku gatsu*
just: it's just arrived *chohdo tsuki-mashta*
  I've just got one left *hitotsu dake nokotte imasu*

K

key *kih; kagi*
keyboard *kihbohdo*
kidney *jinzoh*
kilo *kiro*
kilometer *kiromehtoru*
kimono *kimono*
kiss (noun) *kisu*
kitchen *daidokoro*
kitchen towel *fukin*
knee *hiza*
knife *naifu*
knit *amu*
know: I don't know *shirimasen*
Korea *Kankoku*
  North Korea *Kita Chohsen*
  South Korea *Daikanminkoku*
Korean (person) *kankoku jin*
  (adj) *kankoku no*

L

label *raberu*
lace *rehsu*
lady *fujin/jyoseh*
lake *mizu-umi*
lamb *kohitsuji*
lamp *ranpu; denki stando*
lampshade *denki stando no kasa*
land (noun) *tochi*
  (verb) *chakuriku suru*
language *gengo*
laptop (computer) *(nohto) pasokon*
large *ohkih*
last (final) *saigo (no)*
  last week *senshu*
  last month *sen getsu*
  at last! *tsui ni*
late: it's getting late *moh osoi desu*
  the train is late *densha wa okurete imasu*
laugh *warai*
laundromat *koin-randorih*
laundry (place) *kurihningu ya*
  (dirty clothes) *sentaku-mono*
laundry detergent *senzai*
law (field of study) *hohritsu/hohgaku*
lawyer *bengoshi*
laxative *gezai*
lazy: he is lazy *kare wa namake-mono desu*
leaf *ha/happa*
leaflet *chirashi*
learn *narau/manabu*

leather *kawa*
leave (go away) *deru/saru*
  (object) *nokosu*
lecture *kohgi*
lecturer *kohshi*
left (not right) *hidari*
  turn left *hidari ni magatte kudasai*
left luggage *tenimotsu azukarisho* (locker) *rokkah*
leg *ashi*
leisure *reyjah*
lemon *remon*
lemonade *remonehdo*
length *nagasa*
lens *renzu*
less: less than ... *...yori sukunai*
lesson *jugyoh*
letter *tegami*
lettuce *retasu*
library *toshokan*
license *menkyo*
license plate *nambah-purehto*
life *seikatsu*
lift: could you give me a lift? *nosete kure-masenka*
light (not heavy) *karui*
  (not dark) *akarui*
light meter *roshutsukei*
lighter *raitah*
lighter fuel *raitah no gasu*
like: I like ... *...ga suki desu*
  I don't like it *suki dewa arimasen*
  I'd like ... *...o onegai shimasu; ...o kudasai*
lime (fruit) *raimu*
line (subway) *sen*
  (mark) *retsu*
  (position) *narabu*
lip balm *rippu-kurihmu*
lipstick *kuchi-beni*
liqueur *rikyu-ru*
liquor store *saka ya*
list *risuto*
literature (field of study) *bungaku*
liter *rittoru*
litter *gomikuzu*
little (small) *chihsai*
  just a little *hon no sukoshi*
liver *kanzoh*
living room *ima/ribingu*
lobster *ise-ebi*
lollipop *boh tsuki kyandeh*
long *nagai*
  how long does it take? *dono kurai kakari masuka*
lost property *wasure-mono*

lot: a lot *takusan*
 not a lot *ohku arimasen*
loud: in a loud voice
 ohgoe de
lounge *raunji*
love (noun) *ai*
 (verb) *ai suru*
lover *koibito*
low *hikui*
luck *un* **good luck!**
 guddo rakku/ganbatte
luggage *tenimotsu*
luggage rack
 nimotsu-dana
lunch *chu-shoku*

M

magazine *zasshi*
mail (verb) *yu-soh suru*
 (noun) *yu-bin-butsu*
mail carrier *yu-bin haitatsu nin*
mailbox (private) *yu-bimbako*
 (public) *posuto*
make *tsukuru*
make-up *keshohhin*
man *otoko; danseh; hito*
manager *manehjyah*
map *chizu* **a map of Tokyo**
 Tohkyoh no chizu
March *san gatsu*
margarine *mahgarin*
market *ichiba*
marmalade *mahmarehdo*
married: I'm married
 kekkon shite imasu
martial arts *budoh*
mascara *masukara*
massage *massahji*
mat (straw) *tatami*
match (light) *macchi*
 (sports) *shiai*
material (cloth) *kiji*
matter: what's the matter? *doh shimashitaka*
mattress *mattoresu*
May *go gatsu*
may be *tabun*
me: it's me *watashi desu*
 it's for me *watashi no desu*
 give it to me *watashi ni kudasai*
meal *shokuji*
meat *niku*
mechanic *kikai gishi*
medicine (tablets, etc.) *kusuri*
 (field of study) *igaku*
meeting *mihtingu; kaigi*
melon *meron*
memory (computer) *memori*

men (bathroom) *dansei yoh to-ee-reh*
menu *menyu*
message *messehji*
midday *shohgo*
middle: in the middle
 mannaka ni
midnight *mayonaka*
milk *gyu-nyu; miruku*
million *hyaku-man*
mine: it's mine *watashi no (mono) desu*
mineral water
 mineraru wohtah
minute *fun*
mirror *kagami*
mistake *machigai*
 I made a mistake
 machigai-mashita
modem *modem*
mom *okahsan*
monastery *shu-dohin*
Monday *getsuyoh bi*
money *okane*
monkey *saru*
month *tsuki/...gatsu*
monument *kinenhi*
moon *tsuki*
moped *tansha*
more *motto*
morning *asa*
 good morning
 ohayo gozaimasu
 in the morning *asa ni*
mosaic *mozaiku*
mosquito *ka*
mother *okahsan*
 my mother *haha*
motorboat *mohtah-bohto*
motorcycle *ohtobai*
Mount Fuji *fujisan*
mountain *yama*
 mountain climbing *tozan*
mouse (animal) *nezumi*
 (computer) *mausu*
mouth *kuchi*
move *ugoku*
 don't move! *ugokanaide*
 (house) *hikkosu*
movie *eiga*
movie theater *eiga kan*
Mr., Mrs., Ms. *-san*
much: not much *sukoshi*
 much better *zutto ih desu*
mug *kappu*
museum *hakubutsu kan*
mushroom *kinoko*
music *ongaku*
musical instrument *gakki*
musician *ongakuka*

mussels *mu-rugai*
mustache *kuchi hige*
mustard *karashi*
my: my key(s) *watashi no kagi*
mythology *shinwa*

N

nail (metal) *kugi*
 (finger) *tsume*
nail file *nehru-fairu*
nail polish *manikyua*
name *namae*
 my name is ... *watashi no namae wa... desu*
napkin *oshibori; napukin*
narrow *semai*
near: near the door
 doa no chikaku
 near London
 Rondon no chikaku
necessary *hitsuyoh*
neck *kubi*
necklace *nekkuresu*
need (verb) *iru* **I need ...**
 watashi wa... ga irimasu
 ... are needed
 ...ga hitsuyoh desu
needle *hari*
negative (photo) *nega*
neither: neither of them
 dochira mo... masen
 neither ... nor ...
 mo... mo...masen
nephew *oi*
never *kesshite*
new *atarashih*
New Zealand *Nyu-jihrando*
New Zealander (person)
 nyu-jihrando jin
news *nyu-su*
newspaper *shinbun*
newsstand *shinbun ya*
next *tsugi* **next week** *raishu*
 next month *rai getsu*
nice *suteki (na)*
niece *mei*
night *yoru* **two nights** (stay in hotel) *ni haku*
nightclub *naito-kurabu*
nightdress *nemaki*
nine *kyu*
nineteen *jyu-kyu*
ninety *kyu-jyu*
no (response) *ihe*
 I have no money
 okane wa arimasen
 no entry *shin-nyu kinshi*
 no problem *ihdesuyo*
noisy *urusai; yakamashih*

nonsmoking (section)
  kin-en seki
noodles *men rui*
north *kita*
Northern Ireland
  Kita Airurando
nose *hana*
not: not today
  kyoh dewa arimasen
  he is not here
  kare wa koko ni imasen
  not that one
  sore dewa arimasen
notepad *nohto*
nothing *nanimo*
novel *shohsetsu*
November *jyu-ichi gatsu*
now *ima*
nowhere *dokonimo*
number (numeral) *su-ji*
  (telephone) *bangoh*
nurse *kangoshi*
nut (fruit) *kurumi*
  (for bolt) *natto*

O

occasionally *tama ni*
ocean *umi*
o'clock: ... o'clock *...ji*
October *jyu gatsu*
octopus *tako*
of *...no* **the name of the**
  street *michi no namae*
office *jimusho*
  office worker *kaisha in*
often *yoku/tabi tabi*
oil *oiru; sekiyu*
ointment *nankoh*
okay *okkeh*
old (thing) *furui*
  (person) *toshi o totta*
olive *orihbu*
omelet *omuretsu*
on *ue* **on the table**
  tehburu no ue ni
one (numeral) *ichi*
  (+ noun) *hitotsu (no)*
one way *ippoh tsu-koh*
one-way (ticket) *katamichi*
onion *tamanegi*
only *...dake*
open (adj) *aita* (verb) *akeru*
  what time do you open?
  nanji ni akimasuka
opening times (museums/
  libraries) *kaikan jiman;*
  (stores/restaurants)
  eigyoh jikan
operating room
  shujyutsu shitsu

or *soretomo/aruiwa*
orange (color) *orenji-iro (no)*
  (fruit) *orenji*
orange juice *orenj jyusu*
orchestra *ohkesutora*
order (noun) *chu-mon; ohdah*
ordinary *futsu-no*
our *watashi tachi no*
  it's ours *watashi tachi no*
  (mono) *desu*
out: he's out *kare wa*
  gaishutsu shite imasu
outside *soto*
over (more than) *ijyoh*
  (above) *ue*
  over there *mukoh*
overpass *rittai kohsa*
overtake *oikosu*
oyster *kaki*

P

Pacific Ocean *Taiheiyoh*
pacifier (for baby) *oshaburi*
pack of cards
  kahdo hitokumi
package (parcel) *kozutsumi*
packet *pakku*
  a packet of ... *...hitohako*
padlock *nankinjoh*
page *pehji*
pain *itai; itami*
paint (noun) *penki*
painting (hobby)
  e o kaku koto
pair *futatsu (no)/ittsui (no)*
  a pair of shoes
  kutsu issoku
pajamas *pajama* (traditional
  Japanese) *yukata*
Pakistan *Pakistan*
Pakistani (person) *pakistan*
  jin (adj) *pakistan no*
pale (face) *kaoiro ga warui*
  (color) *usui*
pancakes *pankehki*
pants *pantsu; zubon*
pantyhose *sutokkingu; taitsu*
paper *kami*
  (newspaper) *shinbun*
pardon? *e? nan desuka*
parents *ryohshin*
park (noun) *kohen*
  (verb) *chu-sha suru*
parka *anorakku*
parking: no parking
  chuusha kinshi
  parking space *shako*
parking lot *chusha jyo*
party (celebration) *pahtih*
  (group) *dantai*

  (political) *seitoh*
passenger *ryokyaku*
passport *pasupohto*
  passport control
  (entering) *nyu-koku shinsa*
  (leaving) *shukkoku shinsa*
path *komichi*
patient (in the hospital)
  byoh-nin
pavement *hodoh*
pay *harau*
  where can I pay?
  doko de harae masuka
payment *shiharai*
peach *momo/pihchi*
peanuts *pihnatsu*
pear *nashi*
pearl *shinju/pahru*
peas *mame*
pedestrian *hokohsha*
pen *pen*
pencil *enpitsu*
pencil sharpener
  enpitsu kezuri
peninsula *hantoh*
penknife *chihsai naifu*
penpal *penparu*
people *hitobito*
  (nation) *kokumin*
pepper (condiment) *koshoh*
  (vegetable) *pihman*
peppermints
  hakka-dorop/minto
per *...ni tsuki*
  per person *hitori ni tsuki*
perfect *kanzen (na)*
perfume *kohsui*
perhaps *tabun*
perm *pahma*
petticoat *pechikohto*
pharmacy *yakkyoku*
phonecard *tereka;*
  terehon cahdo
photocopier *kopihki*
photocopy *kopih*
photograph (noun) *shashin*
  (verb) *shashin o toru*
photographer *shashinka*
phrase book *furehzubukku*
physics (field of study)
  butsuri
piano *piano*
pickpocket *suri*
  I've been pickpocketed
  surare mashita
picnic *pikunikku*
piece *hitokire/hitotsu*
pig *buta*
pillow *makura*
pilot *pairotto*
pin *pin*

pine (tree) *matsu*
pineapple *painappuru*
pink *pinku*
pipe (for smoking) *paip*
(for water) *suidohkan*
pizza *piza*
place *basho*
plants *shokubutsu*
plastic *purasuchikku*
plastic bag *binihru-bukuro*
plate *sara*
platform *purrattohohmu*
play (theater) *geki/shibai*
pleasant *kimochi no ih*
please (give me)
(o) onegai shimasu
(please do) *dohzo*
plug (electrical) *konsento*
(sink) *sen*
plumber *haikankoh*
pocket *poketto*
poison *doku*
police *kehsatsu*
police officer *kehsatsu kan;*
omawarisan
police report *tsuh-hoh*
police station *kehsatsu sho*
politics *seiji*
pond *ike*
poor *mazushih*
(bad quality)
shitsu ga warui
pop music *poppu*
pork *butaniku/pohku*
port (harbor) *minato*
porter *pohtah* (train
station) *akaboh*
possible *kanoh*
postcard *hagaki*
poster *posutah*
post office *yu-bin kyoku*
potato *poteto*
poultry *toriniku*
powder *kona/paudah*
pregnant: I'm pregnant
ninshin shite imasu
prescription *shohohsen*
pretty (beautiful)
kireh (na)
price *nedan*
priest (Shintoh) *kannushi*
(Buddhist) *obohsan*
(Christian) *bokushi*
printer *purintah*
private *kojin (no)*
problem *mondai*
what's the problem?
doh shimashtaka
produce market *yao ya*
**profession: what's your
profession?**

goshokugyoh wa
professor *kyohjyu*
profits *ri-eki*
public *ohyake*
pull *hiku*
puncture *panku*
purple *murasaki*
purse *saifu*
push *osu*
put *oku*

Q

quality *shitsu*
question *shitsumon*
quick *hayai*
quiet *shizuka (na)*
quite (fairly) *kanari*
(fully) *sukkari*

R

rabbit *usagi*
radiator *rajiehtah*
radio *rajio*
radish *daikon*
railroad *tetsudoh*
rain *ame*
raincoat *reinkohto*
raisins *hoshi-budoh/rehzun*
rare (uncommon) *mezurashih*
(steak) *re-ah*
rat *dobu-nezumi*
raw *nama (no)*
razor blades *kamisori*
no ha
read *yomu*
reading *dokusho*
reading lamp
dokusho ranpu
ready *yohi ga deki-mashita*
ready meals
kakoh shokuhin
rear lights *tehru-ranpu*
receipt *reshihto/ryohshyu-sho*
reception *uketsuke*
record (music) *rekohdo*
(sports, etc.) *kiroku*
record player
rekohdo-purehyah
red *aka*
refreshments *nomimono*
refrigerator *reizohko*
registered mail
kakitome yu-bin
relatives (family) *shinseki*
relax *yukkuri suru*
religion *shu-kyoh*
remember *oboete iru*
I don't remember
oboete imasen

rent (verb) *kasu*
repairs *shu-ri*
report (noun) *hohkoku sho;*
repohto
reservation *yoyaku*
rest (remainder) *sono hoka*
(relaxation) *yasumu*
restaurant *resutoran*
retailer *tenshu*
return (come back) *kaeru*
(give back) *kaesu*
rice (uncooked) *kome*
(cooked) *gohan*
rice cooker *sui-hanki*
rich (person) *kanemochi (no)*
(food) *kotteri shita*
right (correct) *tadashih*
that's right *sohdesu*
(direction) *migi*
turn right
migi ni magatte kudasai
ring (to call) *denwa suru*
(wedding, etc.) *yubiwa*
ripe *jukushita*
river *kawa*
road *dohro; michi*
roasted *rohsuto shita*
rock (stone) *ishi* (music) *rokku*
roll (bread) *rohru-pan*
roof *yane*
room *heya*
(space) *basho/supehsu*
rope *tsuna/rohpu*
rose *bara*
round (circular) *marui*
it's my round
watashi no ban desu
round-trip (ticket) *ohfuku*
route (bus, etc.) *sen*
rowboat *bohto*
rubber (eraser) *keshigomu*
(material) *gomu*
ruby (stone) *rubih*
rug (mat) *shikimono*
(blanket) *mohfu*
ruins *haikyo/iseki*
ruler (for drawing) *johgi*
rum *ramu*
run (person) *hashiru*
Russia *Roshia*
Russian (person) *roshia jin*
(adj) *roshia no*

S

sad *kanashih*
safe *anzen (na)*
safety pin *anzen-pin*
sailboat *hansen*
sake *osake*
salad *sarada*

salami *sarami*
sale (at reduced prices) *sehru*
sales (figures) *uri age*
salmon *sake*
salt *shio*
same: the same dress
  onaji doresu
  the same people
  onaji hito
  same again please
  onajino o moh hitotsu
  onegai shimasu
sand *suna*
sand dunes *sakyu*
sandals *sandaru*
sandwich *sando icchi*
sanitary napkins
  seiriyoh napkin
satellite TV *sateraito terebi/*
  ehseh terebi
Saturday *doyoh bi*
sauce *sohsu*
saucepan *nabe*
sauna *sauna*
sausage *sohsehji*
say *yu* what did you say?
  nan to iware mashitaka
  How do you say ... in
  Japanese? *...wa nihongo de*
  nanto ihmasuka
scarf *sukahfu*
school *gakkoh*
science (field of study)
  kagaku
scissors *hasami*
Scotland *Sukottorando*
Scottish *sukottorando no*
screen (computer, etc.)
  gamen
screen door (ryokan) *fusuma*
screen window
  (ryokan) *shoji*
screw *neji*
screwdriver *neji-mawashi/*
  sukuryu doraibah
scroll *makimono*
seafood *shifudo*
seafood shop *sakana ya*
seat *seki*
seat belt *shihto-beruto*
second (adj) *nibamme (no)*
  (time) *byoh*
secretary *hisho*
see *miru*
  I can't see *miemasen*
  I see (understand) *soh*
  desuka/wakarimashita
self-employed *ji-eigyoh*
sell *uru*
seminar *zemi/seminah*
send *okuru*

separate *betsu (no)*
separated (from husband,
  etc.) *wakareta*
September
  kyu gatsu
serious (situation) *jyu-dai (na)*
  (person) *majime (na)*
set (in theater) *setto*
seven *shichi/nana*
seventeen *jyu-shichi/*
  jyu-nana
seventy *nana-jyu*
several *ikutsuka (no)*
sew *nuu*
shampoo *shanpu*
shave (noun) *hige-sori*
  (verb) *hige o soru*
shaving foam
  hige-soriyoh sekken
shawl *shohru*
she *kanojo*
sheep *hitsuji*
sheet *shihtsu*
shell *kai/kaigara*
sherry *sherih*
Shinto (adj) *shintoh no*
Shintoism *shintoh*
ship *fune*
shirt *shatsu*
shoe polish *kutsu-zumi*
shoe store *kutsu ya*
shoelaces *kutsu-himo*
shoes *kutsu*
shrimp *shiba-ebi*
  jumbo shrimp *ise-ebi*
shopping *kaimono/shoppingu*
  to go shopping *kaimono*
  ni iku shopping cart
  shoppingu kahto
short (object) *mijikai*
  (person) *(se ga) hikui*
shorts *hanzubon/shohtsu*
shoulder *kata*
shower (bath) *shawah*
  (rain) *niwaka ame*
shower gel *shawah jeru*
shrimp *ebi*
shrine *jinja*
shutter (window) *amado*
  (camera) *shattah*
siblings *go kyohdai*
  my siblings *kyohdai*
sick (ill) *byohki* I feel sick
  kimochi ga warui desu
side (edge) *hashi*
  I'm on her side *watashi*
  wa kanojo no mikata desu
side mirror *saido mirah*
sidelights *saido-raito*
sights: the sights of ...
  ...no kenbutsu

sightseeing *kankoh*
silk *kinu*
silver (color) *giniro (no)*
  (metal) *gin*
simple *kantan (na)/*
  shinpuru (na)
sing *utau*
single (one) *hitotsu*
  (unmarried) *dokushin*
single room *shinguru ru-mu*
sink (kitchen) *nagashi*
sister (older) *ane*
  (younger) *imohto*
six *roku*
sixteen *jyu-roku*
sixty *roku-jyu*
size (clothes) *saizu*
skid (verb) *suberu*
skin cleanser
  kurenjingu-kurihm
skirt *sukahto*
sky *sora*
sleep (noun) *suimin*
  (verb) *nemuru*
  to go to sleep *neru*
sleeping bag *nebukuro*
sleeping pill *suimin-yaku*
sleeve *sode*
slippers *surippa*
slow *osoi*
small *chihsai*
smell (noun) *nioi* (verb) *niou*
smile (noun) *hohoemi*
  (verb) *hohoemu*
smoke (noun) *kemuri*
  (verb) *tabako o su*
smoking (section)
  kitsu-en seki
snack *sunakku*
snow *yuki*
so: so good *totemo ih*
  not so much ...
  sore hodo... dewa arimasen
soaking solution
  (for contact lenses)
  kontaktoyoh hozoneki
soap *sekken*
soccer *sakkah* (ball) *bohru*
socks *kutsushita*
soda water *sohdasui*
soft *yawarakai*
soft lenses *softo-renzu*
soil (earth) *tsuchi*
somebody *dareka*
somehow *nantoka/dohnika*
something *nanika*
sometimes *tokidoki*
somewhere *dokoka*
son *musuko san*
  my son *musuko*
song *uta*

soon *moh sugu*
sorry! *gomennasai*
  I'm sorry *sumimasen*
soup *supu*
south *minami*
South Africa *Minami Afurika*
South African
  (person) *minami afurika jin*
  (adj) *minami afurika no*
souvenir *omiyage*
spade (shovel) *suki*
  (cards) *supehdo*
spares *yobi-hin*
spark plug *tenka-puragu*
speak *hanasu*
  do you speak ...?
  ...o hanashi-masuka
  I don't speak ...
  ...wa hanashimasen
speed *supihdo*
spider *kumo*
spoon *supuun*
sports *supohtsu*
sprain *nenza*
spring (season) *haru*
  (mechanical) *bane*
square (in town) *hiroba*
stadium *stajiamu*
stage (in theater) *butai*
staircase *kaidan*
stairs *kaidan*
stamps *kitte*
stapler *hochikisu*
star *hoshi* (film) *sutah*
start *shuppatsu/sutahto*
  (verb) *shuppatsu suru*
statement (to police) *hohkoku sho*
station *eki*
statue *dohzoh*
steal *nusumu*
  it's been stolen *nusumare-mashita*
steamed (food) *mushita*
steps *kaidan*
stereo: personal stereo *uohkman*
stockings *sutokkingu*
stomach *onaka*
stomachache *fukutsu*
stop (verb) *tomaru*
  (bus stop) *basutei*
  stop! *tomare*
store *mise*
storm *arashi*
stove (kitchen) *renji*
straight ahead *massugu*
strawberry *ichigo/sutoroberih*
stream *ogawa*
street *michi/dohro*

string (cord) *himo/kohdo*
  (guitar, etc.) *gen*
stroller *uba-guruma*
student *gakusei*
stupid *baka*
suburbs *kohgai*
subway *chikatetsu*
subway station *chikatetsu no eki*
sugar *satoh*
suit (noun) *su-tsu*
  (verb) *au/niau*
  it suits you *anata ni niaimasu*
suitcase *su-tsu kehsu*
summer *natsu*
sun *taiyoh*
sunbathe *nikkohyoku*
sunburn *hiyake*
Sunday *nichiyoh bi*
sunglasses *sangurasu*
sunny: it's sunny *hi ga dete imasu/tenki ga ih desu*
suntan *hiyake*
suntan lotion *hiyake rohshon*
supermarket *su-pah*
supplement (for fares) *tsuika ryohkin*
suppository *zayaku*
surname *myohji*
suspenders (pants) *zubon-tsuri*
sweat (noun) *ase*
  (verb) *ase o kaku*
sweatshirt *torehnah*
sweet (not sour) *amai*
  (candy) *kyandih*
swim cap *sui-ei boh*
swimming *suiei*
  swimsuit *mizuigi*
  swimming pool *suimingu pu-ru*
  swim trunks *suiei-pantsu*
switch *suicchi*
syringe *chu-sha ki*
syrup *shiroppu*

T

table *tehburu*
tablet *jyohzai*
Taiwan *Taiwan*
take *noru*
  I want to take the train *densha ni noritai desu*
  can I take it with me? *motte itte mo ih desuka*
  we'll take it *kore ni shimasu*
take-out *mochi-kaeri*

takeoff *ririku*
talcum powder *tarukamu-paudah*
talk (noun) *hanashi*
  (verb) *hanasu*
tall *takai*
tampon *tanpon*
tangerine *mikan*
tapestry *tapesutorih*
tax: including tax *zeikomi*
taxi *takushih*
taxi stand *takushih noriba*
tea (Western) *kohcha*
  (Japanese) *ocha*
teacher *sensei*
teahouse *chamise*
team *chihmu*
telephone (noun) *denwa*
  (verb) *denwa suru/denwa o kakeru*
telephone booth *denwa bokkusu*
telephone call *denwa*
telephone number *denwa bangoh*
television *terebi*
temperature *ondo*
  (fever) *netsu*
temple *tera*
ten *jyu*
ten thousand *ichi man*
tennis *tenisu*
tent *tento*
terminal (airport) *tahminaru*
test (medical) *kensa*
than *yori*
thank (verb) *kansha suru*
  thank you *arigatoh*
  thank you very much *arigatoh gozaimasu*
that: that bus *ano basu*
  what's that? *a-re wa nan desuka*
  I think that ... *...to omoimasu*
theater *gekijyoh*
their: their room(s) *karera no heya*
  it's theirs *karera no (mono) desu*
them: it's them *karera desu*
  it's for them *karera no desu* **give it to them** *karera ni agenasai*
theme park *tehma pahku*
then *sore kara/soshite*
there (near you) *soko*
  (over there) *asoko*
  there is/are ... *...ga/wa arimasu/imasu*

there isn't/aren't ...
...*ga/wa arimasen/imasen*
is there ...? ...*ga/wa arimasuka/imasuka*
these: these things *korera no mono/kore*
these are mine *korera wa watashi no (mono) desu*
they *karera*
thick *atsui*
thief *yatoh*
thin *usui;* (person) *yaseta*
thing (abstract) *koto* (concrete) *mono*
think *omou/kangaeru*
I think so *soh omoimasu*
I'll think about it *kangaete mimasu*
third *sanbamme*
thirsty: I'm thirsty *nodo ga kawaite imasu*
thirteen *jyu-san*
thirty *san-jyu*
this: this bus *kono basu*
what's this? *kore wa nan desuka*
this is Mr. ... *kochira wa...-san desu*
those: those things *sorera no mono/sore*
those are his *sorera wa kare no (mono) desu*
thousand *sen*
ten thousand (ichi) *man*
three *san*
throat *nodo*
through: through Tokyo *Tohkyoh keiyu*
thumb tack *oshi pin*
thunderstorm *raiu*
Thursday *mokuyoh bi*
ticket *chiketto*
tie (noun) *nekutai* (verb) *musubu*
time *jikan*
what's the time? *ima nanji desuka*
to be on time *yotei dohri*
timetable *jikoku-hyoh*
tip (money) *chippu* (end) *saki*
tire *taiya*
tired *tsukareta*
I feel tired *tsukare-mashita*
tissues *tisshu*
to: to England *Igirisu e*
to the station *eki e*
toast *tohsuto*

tobacco *tabako*
today *kyoh*
toe *ashi no tsumasaki*
tofu shop *tofu ya*
together *issho ni*
toilet *to-ee-reh*
toilet paper *toiretto pehpah*
tomato *tomato*
tomato juice *tomato jyusu*
tomorrow *ashita*
tongue *shita*
tonic *tonikku*
tonight *konya*
too (also) *mo* (excessive) *-sugiru*
tooth *ha*
toothache *ha-ita*
toothbrush *haburashi*
toothpaste *hamigaki*
torch *kaichu dentoh*
tour *tsuah*
tourist *ryokoh-sha*
tourist information center *kankoh an-naijyo*
towel *taoru*
tower *tawah/toh*
town *machi*
town hall *shiyakusho*
toy *omocha*
track suit *undoh-gi*
tractor *torakutah*
tradition *dentoh*
traffic *kohtsuu*
traffic jam *kohtsuu-jyu-tai*
traffic lights *shingoh*
trailer (for car) *torehrah*
train *densha*
translate *honyaku suru*
transmission (for car) *toransumisshon*
travel agency *ryokoh dairi den*
tray *obon/toreh*
traveling *ryokoh*
tree *ki*
truck *torakku*
trunk (car) *toranku*
try *yatte miru/tamesu*
Tuesday *kayoh bi*
tunnel *tonneru*
tweezers *pinsetto*
twelve *jyu-ni*
twenty *ni-jyu*
twin room *tsuin ru-mu*
two *ni*
type *taipu*
what type of ... do you have? *donna taipu no... desuka*

U

umbrella *kasa*
uncle *ojisan*
under *shita*
underwear *shitagi*
university *daigaku*
until ... ...*ma-de*
unusual *mezurashih*
up *ue* (upward) *ue ma-de*
urgent *kyu* (na)/*isogi no*
it's urgent *kinkyu desu*
us: it's us *watashi tachi desu*
it's for us *watashi tachi no desu*
give it to us *watashi tachi ni kudasai*
use (noun) *shiyoh* (verb) *tsukau* **it's no use** *yakuni tachimasen/tsukae masen*
useful *yakuni tatsu/benri na*
usual *itsumo no*
usually *itsumo*

V

vacancy (room) *akibeya*
vacation *yasumi*
vacuum cleaner *sohjiki*
vacuum flask *mahohbin*
valley *tani*
valve *ben*
vanilla *banira*
vanity box (ryokan) *kyodai*
vase *kabin*
veal *koushi no niku*
vegetables *yasai*
vegetarian *bejitarian*
vehicle *kuruma*
very *totemo*
very much *totemo*
vest *chokki/besuto*
video games *bideo gehmu*
video tape *bideo tehpu*
view *keshiki/nagame*
viewfinder *fainda*
villa *bessoh*
village *mura*
vinegar *su*
violin *baiorin*
visa *biza*
visit (noun) *hohmon* (verb) *hohmon suru*
visitor *hohmonsha* (tourist) *ryokoh sha*
vitamin *bitaminzai*
vodka *uokkah*
voice *koe*
voicemail *boisu mehru*

W

wait *matsu*
waiter *uehtah*
   waiter! *sumimasen*
waiting room *machiai shitsu*
waitress *uehtoresu*
Wales *Uehruzu*
walk (noun: stroll) *sanpo*
   (verb) *sanpo suru/aruku*
   to go for a walk *sanpo
   ni iku*
wall *kabe*
wallet *saifu*
war *sensoh*
ward *byohtoh*
wardrobe *yohfuku-dansu*
warm *atatakai*
was: I was
   watashi wa...deshita
   he was *kare wa...deshita*
   she was *kanojo wa...deshita*
   it was *sore wa...deshita*
washing machine *sentaku ki*
wasp *suzume-bachi*
watch (wristwatch) *udedokei*
   (verb) *miru*
water *mizu*
waterfall *taki*
wave (noun) *nami*
   (verb) *te o furu*
we *watashi tachi*
weather *tenki*
website *Web saito*
wedding *kekkonshiki*
Wednesday *suiyoh bi*
week *shu*
welcome! *yohkoso*
well: I don't feel well
   chohshi ga warui desu
Welsh *Uehruzu (no)*
were: we were
   watashi tachi wa...deshita
   you were *anata wa...
   deshita* (sing. informal)
   kimi wa...deshita
   they were
   karera wa...deshita
west *nishi*
   the West *seiyoh*
Western-style *yohfuu*
Westerner *seiyoh jin*
wet *nureta*
what? *nani/nandesuka*
wheel (of vehicle) *sharin*
   (steering) *handoru*
wheelchair *kurumaisu*
when? *itsu*
where? *doko*
which? (of two) *dochira*
   (of more than two) *dore*

whisky *uisukih*
white *shiro*
who? *dare/donata* (formal)
whom: with whom? *dare/
   donata to*
why? *naze/dohshite*
wide *hiroi*
wife *okusan*
   my wife *tsuma*
wind *kaze*
window *mado*
windshield *furonto garasu*
wine *wain/budohshu*
wine list *wain risuto*
wing *tsubasa/hane*
winter *fuyu*
with (together with)
   ...to issho ni
   I'll go with you
   a nata to issho ni ikimasu
   (using) *...de*
   with a pen *pen de*
   with sugar *satoh iri*
without *...nashi (de)*
   without sugar
   satoh nashide
witness (person)
   shoh nin
woman *onna; jyoseh*
women (bathroom) *fujin
   to-ee-reh*
wood *mori/zaimoku*
wool *yohmoh*
word *kotoba*
work (noun) *shigoto*
   (verb) *hataraku*
   it doesn't work
   ugokimasen
worse *motto warui*
worst *saiaku (na)*
wrapping paper
   tsutsumi-gami/hohsohshi
wrench *spana*
wrist *tekubi*
write *kaku*
writing paper *binsen*
wrong: it is wrong
   machigatte imasu

X, Y

x-ray *rentogen*
year *nen*
yellow *ki iro*
yen *yen*
yes *hai*
yesterday *kinoh*
yet *moh*
   not yet *mada*
yogurt *yohguruto*
you (sing. formal) *anata*

   (sing. informal) *kimi*
   (plural formal) *anata-gata*
   (plural informal) *kimitachi*
young *wakai*
your: your shoe(s)
   (formal) *anata no kutsu*
   (informal) *kimi no kutsu*
yours: is this yours?
   (formal) *kore wa anata
   no desuka*
   (informal) *kore, kimi no*
youth hostel *yu-su hosuteru*

Z

zen *zen*
zen Buddhism *zenshu*
zen garden *zendera no niwa*
zipper *chakku/zippah*
zoo *dohbutsuen*

HIRAGANA/KATAKANA TABLES

Japanese is written in three different script systems: *kanji*, *hiragana*, and *katakana* (see p.14). *Kanji* are Chinese pictograms that need to be learned individually, but *hiragana* and *katakana* are "syllabaries," with each character representing a separate syllable. The full syllabaries are given here to help you work out the characters in a particular word. With time, you will become more familiar with the most common characters.

Hiragana

あ a	か ka	さ sa	た ta	な na
い i	き ki	し shi	ち chi	に ni
う u	く ku	す su	つ tsu	ぬ nu
え e	け ke	せ se	て te	ね ne
お o	こ ko	そ so	と to	の no

は ha	ま ma	や ya	ら ra	わ wa
ひ hi	み mi		り ri	
ふ fu	む mu	ゆ yu	る ru	
へ he	め me		れ re	
ほ ho	も mo	よ yo	ろ ro	を wo
				ん n

Katakana

ア a	カ ka	サ sa	タ ta	ナ na
イ i	キ ki	シ shi	チ chi	ニ ni
ウ u	ク ku	ス su	ツ tsu	ヌ nu
エ e	ケ ke	セ se	テ te	ネ ne
オ o	コ ko	ソ so	ト to	ノ no

ハ ha	マ ma	ヤ ya	ラ ra	ワ wa
ヒ hi	ミ mi		リ ri	
フ fu	ム mu	ユ yu	ル ru	
ヘ he	メ me		レ re	
ホ ho	モ mo	ヨ yo	ロ ro	ヲ wo
				ン n

There are two signs (" and °) that are used to add additional sounds to the characters in the syllabaries. For example, the character ヒ *hi* can become ピ *pi*, て *te* can become で *de*, and ほ *ho* can become ぽ *po*.

In addition, a long dash (–) is used to lengthen *katakana* syllables. For example, the katakana character テ *te* is lengthened to テー *teh* by adding this dash, used in a word such as テーブル *tehburu* (*table*); and the character ピ *pi* is lengthened to ピー *pih*, used in a word such as コピー *kopih* (*photocopy*).

Acknowledgments

The publisher would like to thank the following for their help in the preparation of this book. In Japan: Hajime Fukase, Keihin Kyuko Bus Co., Ltd, Takao Abe, Seitoku Kinen Kaigakan, Koei drug, Ichinoyu group, East Japan Railway Company (JR), East Japan Marketing & Communications, Inc. (JR Higashi Nihon Kikaku), Kenichi Miyokawa, Naoki Ogawa, Yumiko Nagahari. In the UK: Capel Manor College, Toyota (GB), Magnet Kitchens Kentish Town, Canary Wharf plc, St. Giles College, Yo! Sushi.

Language content for Dorling Kindersley by **g-and-w publishing**
Managed by **Jane Wightwick**

Picture research: **Hugh Schermuly, Hajime Fukase**

Picture credits

Key: *t = top; b = bottom; l = left; r = right; c = center; A = above; B = below*

p2/3 **DK Images:** *br;* p4/5 **Laura Knox:** *cl;* p14/15 **DK Images:** *Paul Bricknell cAl;* **Ingram Image Library:** *cbl, cAr;* p16/17 **Ingram Image Library:** *ctr;* p18/19 **DK Images:** *David Murray tr;* p24/25 **Takehisa Yano:** *cbl,* **Ingram Image Library:** *tcr;* p28/29 **DK Images:** *John Bulmer tcr; Dave King cr;* **Ingram Image Library:** *bcr;* p30/31 **Alamy RF:** *Comstock Images bcl;* **DK Images:** *cl;* p34/35 **iStockphoto.com:** *Nicolas cra;* p36/37 **DK Images:** *cbr;* **Dreamstime.com:** *Slobodan Mračina ca;* **iStockphoto.com:** *Nicolas c;* p38/39 **Takehisa Yano:** *bl-r, ĉɔr, cr;* p40/41 **Takehisa Yano:** *bl, tcr, cAr, cr, cBr, cbA, bcr bcrA;* p42/43 **Takehisa Yano:** *bl-r, c, cr, crB;* p44/45 **Courtesy of Toyota (GB):** *c;* p46/47 **Toyota (GB):** *ctr;* **Ingram Image Library:** *cAr;* **Takehisa Yano:** *cr, cl, cAl;* p48/49 **Takehisa Yano:** *c, bl, cr;* p50/51 **Takehisa Yano:** *tcr;* **Alamy:** *Peter Titmuss cr;* p52/53 **Getty:** *Stone: Kiriko Shirobayashi cl,* **Alamy RF:** *Image Farm Inc cAr;* **Takehisa Yano:** *bl-r, cr, cBr;* p54/55 **Alamy:** *Frank Herholdt bcl; Jackson Smith cBl;* **Alamy RF:** *BananaStock cl; John Foxx c;* **ThinkStock tcr;** **DK Images:** *Andy Crawford bclA;* p56/57 **Takehisa Yano:** *cl, cAl;* **Toyota (GB):** *bl, cBr;* p58/59 **Alamy RF:** *Brand X Pictures cBl; Image Source cAAl;* **DK Images:** *John Heseltine cr;* p60/61 **123RF.com:** *Shutswis c;* **Alamy RF:** *Image Source cAr;* **DK Images:** *Steve Gorton cAAr; Pia Tryde cAr;* p62/63 **DK Images:** *Russell Sadur cBr, Jo Foord cr;* **Takehisa Yano:** *bl-r, c;* **Alamy RF:** *Goodshoot cAr;* p64/65 **Alamy:** *Arcaid bcrA;* **Alamy RF:** *Diana Ninov cAr;* **Ingram Image Library:** *tcr;* p66/67 **Alamy:** *Arcaid cll;* **Ingram Image Library:** *bcr;* **Alamy RF:** *Image Source cr;* **Takehisa Yano:** *bl; p68/69* **Takehisa Yano:** *clAl, clAr, cll, clBl, clBr, ctr, cAr cBr, cbr;* p70/71 **123RF.com:** *Sergey Skripnikov c, cr;* **Dreamstime.com:** *Bombaert c/mouse; Lwi1977 c/flashdrive; Milotus / Magic Mouse is a trademark of Apple Inc., registered in the U.S. and other countries cr/ mouse;* p72/73 **Alamy RF:** *Image Source cAr;* **Comstock Images tcr;** p74/75 **Alamy RF:** *Doug Norman bl;* p76/77 **123RF.com:** *Sergey Skripnikov ca, ca/laptop;* **Dreamstime.com:** *Bombaert cla; Milotus / Magic Mouse is a trademark of Apple Inc., registered in the U.S. and other countries ca/mouse; Lwi1977 c/mouse; bl, bcll, bclll, bcAl, bcAll, cbr;* p80/81 **Getty:** *Taxi / Rob Melnychuk bc;* **Ingram Image Library:** *cAr;* **Xerox UK Ltd:** *tcr;* p82/83 **Alamy:** *wildphotos.com tcr;* **Alamy RF:** *Momentum Creative Group cAl;* **Ingram Image Library:** *cl;* p84/85 **Alamy:** *Brand X Pictures cr;* **Alamy RF:** *SuperStock tr;* **Ingram Image Library:** *crB;* p86/87 **Getty:** *Taxi / Rob Melnychuk tc;* p90/91 **DK Images:** *cl; David Jordan cAr; Stephen Oliver cr;* **Ingram Image Library:** *cBr;* p92/93 **Ingram Image Library:** *cl;* **Alamy RF:** *Pixland cr;* **DK Images:** *Guy Ryecart tr;* p94/95 **Alamy RF:** *ImageState Royalty Free bcr;* **DK Images:** *tcr;* p96/97 **DK Images:** *ctl;* p98/99 **Getty Images:** *Daisuke Morita c;* **Alamy:** *Ian Lambot bl;* p102/103 **Garden Picture Library:** *Marie O'Hara b;* **DK Images:** *tcr; James Young cAAr;* p104/105 **DK Images:** *Bob Langrish cl(6); Jane Burton bcl; Geoff Dann cl(2); Max Gibbs cl(4); Frank Greenaway cl(3); Tracy Morgan c(5);* p106/107 **Getty Images:** *Daisuke Morita cr;* p110/111 **Alamy RF:** *Stockbyte cl;* p112/113 **Ingram Image Library:** *bl;* p116/117 **Takehisa Yano:** *bcl, bc, bcr;* p118/119 **Alamy RF:** *Pixland tcr;* **Corbis:** *Michael S. Yamashita c;* p120/121 **Alamy:** *ImageState / Pictor International cl;* **DK Images:** *bcl;* p122/123 **DK Images:** *Judith Miller / Sparkle Moore at The Girl Can't Help It cl;* p124/125 **DK Images:** *Bob Langrish cl(6); Jane Burton bcl; Geoff Dann cl(2); Max Gibbs cl(4); Frank Greenaway cl(3); Tracy Morgan c(5);* **DK Images:** *Clive Streeter tl;* **Alamy:** *ImageState / Pictor International cl;* **DK Images:** *bcl;* p126/127 **123RF.com:** *Sergey Skripnikov tr, ca;* **Dreamstime.com:** *Bombaert c; Lwi1977 c/flash; Milotus / Magic Mouse is a trademark of Apple Inc., registered in the U.S. and other countries cra;* **Takehisa Yano:** *cl, cll, clll;* **Alamy RF:** *Image Farm Inc bl;* p128 **DK Images:** *Clive Streeter tl.*

All other studio and location images: **Mike Good**